The Buses of
North East Scotland

in colour photographs by John Sinclair

When the mighty Alexander empire was split up into three companies in May 1961, the Northern area had fourteen depots with a number of sub-depots and outstations, extending from Forres down to Dundee. Connected by a network of services for which the timetables showed journeys of over six hours, most of the traffic was local, as exemplified by Buckie based AEC Regal AWG647 (NA60) arriving at Cullen from Portknockie at 4.25pm on 7th March 1966. This was a short working of the "coast" service from Aberdeen to Inverness via Banff and Elgin, which contrasted with the direct route via Huntly, which at that time required a change of bus at Elgin. It was one of 45 AEC Regals which entered service between October 1946 and September 1947. Ten had bodies constructed at Brown Street in Falkirk using Brockhouse kits, and the remainder all metal Alexander bodies built at Stirling, all of which spent their lives in the Northern region apart from one built at Falkirk. NA60 with an Alexander body had been transferred from Elgin Depot in 1963 for less demanding work and was sold in April 1967 to a local builder, Walker, in Banff, and finally scrapped at Turriff.

Stenlake Publishing Ltd

© 2017 John Sinclair
First Published in the United Kingdom, 2017
Stenlake Publishing Limited
54-58 Mill Square, Catrine, KA5 6RD
www.stenlake.co.uk

ISBN 978 1 84033 788 4

Printed by
Berforts, 17 Burgess Road, Hastings, TN35 4NR

The strategically positioned village of Mintlaw was the registered address of Burnett's Motors Ltd which was sold to Northern in January 1967. The business was started by Alexander Burnett in 1925, with a regular service between Mintlaw and Aberdeen established the following year. Over the years, a network of services was developed linking the village and surrounding communities with Peterhead and Turriff, and south to Aberdeen. In 1935, the acquisition of James Burnett of Cuminestown resulted in further routes being introduced from nearby Turriff, where a subsidiary depot was opened. Northern continued to use both depots, with Turriff being closed on 23rd April 1984. The Mintlaw garage, on Longside Road, remained as an operational depot until 15th August 2010. Photographed about to leave for the adjacent village of Stuartfield on 27th May 1970, OJO727 (NA106) was one of three AEC Regal 111s (OJO724/7-8) with crash gear boxes and dual purpose Willowbrook 32 seat bodies purchased from City of Oxford Motor Services in December 1963, and the only one to receive Northern livery. Converted for OMO operation in 1958 by its original owner, and with power-operated doors, it was ideally equipped for rural operation and survived until June 1972, passing into preservation. Now restored to its original livery, it is on display at the Oxford Bus Museum at Long Hanborough.

INTRODUCTION

Monday May 15th 1961 was a notable date in the history of what was then the largest bus company in Scotland, Walter Alexander & Sons Limited, first registered in May 1924. On that day, the Alexander empire was split up into its three geographical components of Midland, Fife and Northern, and on October 3rd I set off with my newly-acquired 35 mm camera to record the changes in the North East of Scotland. I had been visiting the companies and their depots since moving north from Yorkshire to Edinburgh in 1953 and began taking photographs in 1956. From 1958 I routinely travelled round the country hitch hiking, easily able to reach Aberdeen in a day, and by visiting the smaller private companies on the way and using Aberdeen Youth Hostel as a base, had access to all the bus operators in the North East of Scotland.

By 1966 I had a car, and was better able to plan and time visits. Northern was about to embark on a buying spree, acquiring Simpson of Rosehearty, Burnett of Mintlaw and later Mitchell of Luthermuir. I often called into these operators on my regular visits to relatives in the Inverness area, and if necessary could sleep in my car, a favourite place being the picturesque fishing village of Gardenstown. This allowed me to capture on camera the changes which occurred in the operating territory of W. Alexander & Sons (Northern) Ltd during a momentous decade. Between 1973 and 1975, with a young family and a wife who was also a doctor, we used to do locum holiday cover for the GP in Ballater, which entailed professional visits to Balmoral but not to look after The Royal Family. However, it did provide an opportunity to drive around the operating territory of Strachan's Deeside Omnibus Service, which was Northern's first acquisition in May 1965. This book was written to provide a photographic record of these events and what followed in the next few years.

The two smallest Alexander depots in the Northern region were Huntly (code H) and Fyvie (F) which had only eight and six vehicles respectively in an official 1957 allocation list, with Huntly reduced to only six buses in 1960. These were kept in the garage at 1 Deveron Road, just along from the original building which was bought with the business of Robert Gibb on 28th May 1931. However, it was downgraded to the status of an outstation of Elgin Depot in December 1980 with an allocation of four buses, reduced to three after Scotmap in 1983, and finally closed on 8th July 1985, after which the solitary bus was parked at the driver's house. Traditionally, the depot had supplied two front line vehicles for the Aberdeen to Elgin service, two Bedfords for local services from Huntly to Cullen and Keith/Turriff, and half cab single deckers for school runs and duplication. Photographed leaving the depot on 26th August 1963 for the picturesque village of Knock, home of the renowned Knockdhu Distillery, is BWG42 (NW221) new in June 1948 with a SMT body, one of 43 Bedford OBs operated by Alexander. Of these, six passed to Midland and four to Northern, BWG42 being the last of these in service withdrawn in June 1964, becoming a mobile shop, and replaced with a new Bedford VAS (ARG11B), the last new small service bus to enter service with Northern.

Also the last of its class to be withdrawn in the fleet of Alexander (Northern) was WG8111 (NP532) one of 50 (P522-71) Leyland TS8s with Alexander 35 seat bodies new in 1939 for tours and long distance services. By 1961, 21 remained in service with sixteen in the Midland region, one in Fife and four with Northern. All had been rebuilt, many having major modifications carried out, with the Northern body shop at Gairn Terrace being renown for its ingenuity. Only FP539 (F indicating a Fife vehicle) survived until 1964, when it was withdrawn in January having survived in coach livery for use on a tour involving a ferry crossing which required that size of bus. NP532 had just been delicensed when I photographed it at Macduff Depot on 25th August 1963, and was removed in September for sale to a scrap metal dealer in Bellshill. Macduff Depot in Union Road dated back to 1933 and is still in use, having been at various times a sub-depot of Elgin. Throughout the late 1950s and early 1960s it consistently housed 22-23 buses all single deckers with three front line coaches required for the Aberdeen to Inverness service and two for the Aberdeen to Macduff via Aberchirder.

Another Leyland Tiger, probably the last of the "Coronation Coaches" in service, was WG5925 (NP407) photographed arriving in Aberdeen on 26th August 1963 on a morning duplicate run from its home depot of Stonehaven where it was the last pre-war vehicle in service, and already 26 years old. Behind it is Leyland OPS2/1 DMS823 (NPB10) arriving in from its outstation at Tarland. New in 4/37, WG5925 was one of 60 (P351-410) TS7 model with a new design of Alexander body seating 35 passengers in high back seats, and constructed with external sliding doors, although all were converted to folding doors in 1938-9. Originally fitted with half-drop windows these had been replaced with sliding vents, and sunshine roofs had been removed. Twenty nine survived until the company was split up, all being in the Northern region. None had ever operated in Fife. NP405-7/9-10 were scheduled to run until 1964, but 406 saw further use with a contractor in Strachan and the remainder were sold for scrap in December 1963, with 407 and possibly 405 at Montrose continuing in service until October. Some in the southern region were re-engined, either with AEC 7.7 litre engines or the post-war Leyland 7.4 litre E181 version, but all those in the northern area continued with the 8.6 litre Leyland engine.

Facing page upper: However, the final pre-war buses to leave the Northern fleet were Leyland TS7s ASF365/7/78/88 (NP808/10/26/37) the only survivors of the 55 vehicles transferred from SMT to Alexander in December 1949 together with some Dundee area services. New in June 1937 with 35 seat Alexander rear entrance bodies, they had received replacement Duple A bodies in 1951. These had been built as part of an order for six AEC Regals by James Sutherland of Peterhead before the company was sold to Alexander in March 1950, whichsubsequently appeared with Alexander bodies as DMS125-30 (NA99-104.) Allocated to Buckie, Huntly, Macduff and Rosehearty depots respectively for most of their lives, they were used for private hires as well as service work, being withdrawn on 31st May 1964 (NP810) or 30th June 1964 (NP808/26/37) when 27 years old. NP808 was photographed at Elgin Depot on 4th October 1962 still in Bluebird coach livery, and survives in preservation, having been sold to Francis Paterson of Dufftown who operated an infrequent service to Keith via the village of Mulben whose railway station was closed in 1964. When I visited Dufftown in 1970, it was still in daily service and had a COF (MOT) until August 1971.

Facing page lower: Only NP810, and 826 photographed when delicensed at Elgin Depot on 15th September 1964, were repainted into Northern colours. Parked in front is BMS407, one of four Daimler CVD6s BMS405/7/14-5 (ND10/2/9-20) with Burlingham 33 seat bodies which passed to Northern. New in March 1948 it had moved up to Elgin Depot in June 1954 from the Southern region of Alexander with BMS405, and had been extensively rebuilt in August 1959 with replacement of the half-drop windows with sliding vents, removal of the sunshine roof and fitting of a continuous rain strip above the windows. Both were painted into Northern bus livery, but having quiet Daimler engines and coach seats were used for private hires as well as local service work. They always looked immaculate and were not withdrawn until June 1970. The other two were transferred north in May 1956 to Stonehaven and similarly refurbished, but surprisingly painted into Northern's cream and yellow coach colours, although having a similar life to the pair at Elgin Depot. BMS415 survived until December 1970 when it was acquired for preservation, whereas the other nineteen vehicles in the batch which passed to Midland had all been withdrawn during 1965. Parked beside them is Burlingham bodied AEC AMS487 (NA12) in the bus livery applied to this style of body.

One of the most unusual buses to operate in Stonehaven was the prototype Albion Nimbus NSG869 which first ran as a demonstrator with Highland Omnibuses, and my, first ever photograph of a bus was of it in Inverness Bus Station in 1956. With a 32 seat SMT body similar to that designed for a unique bus of integral construction which that company operated (LWS926), it was austere and basic and no other similar bodies appeared. It had a peripatetic existence, and after returning to Albion Motors, was sold to Hutchison of Overtown in September 1956 who kept it for two years, but surprisingly never repainted it out of its original colours. It next appeared in 4/58 with Mitchell's Garage in Stonehaven who used it on their local service from the Market Square to Brickfield. This service was sold to George Reid of Inverurie in November 1959 along with NSG869, and this picture which was given to me by his son shows his father with the bus on the north side of the Market Square.

In October 1962, I came across NSG869 again, now repainted out of Highland colours, and at the same location. A year later, it was sold to the dealer Millburn Motors in Glasgow, passing to another dealer in Macclesfield, Transport Passenger Equipments Ltd, from whom it was purchased by the Staffordshire operator Berresford of Cheddleton, a long-established family company which ran a mixed fleet of unusual vehicles which on withdrawal usually ended up sitting at the side of the yard for many years. It was finally withdrawn in March 1974, but again by chance I came across it while returning from Alton Towers with the family in 1986, now painted red and cream again and awaiting restoration. Finally preserved, it appears regularly at rallies, and by a strange quirk of fate, its present owner keeps it at premises just outside the Yorkshire village of Pocklington where I went to school until the age of twelve.

Another unusual and less likely bus to appear in Stonehaven was a former MacBrayne bus (KGD909) which still retained its mail compartment. It too operated on the town service to Brickfield which was taken over by Invercarron (Stonehaven) Ltd in January 1966. Having photographed it regularly in Skye where for many years it was the regular bus for the mail service from Kilmaluag to Portree via Staffin, I came across it still in MacBrayne livery on 7th July 1967. New in 1952, it was one of 22 Bedford model OLAZ derived from a lorry chassis adapted for island roads and connecting ferries, with a Duple Sportsman body to a design unique to MacBrayne. Twelve of these iconic vehicles had mail compartments from new, with seating capacities which varied over the years, but KGD909 remained a 20 seater for all its life. Operating for Invercarron from December 1965 to September 1968, it then passed to a Fife operator, Petrie of Cupar, who may not have operated it as it ended up in Muir's scrapyard in Kirkcaldy the following year.

The Bedford OB was first introduced in 1939, and by the time the last one entered service in 1951, 12,766 had been built. As such, it was a popular choice for many small Scottish companies operating in rural areas where it was used for both service work and private hires or tours. A typical operator was James Meffan of Parkend, Kirriemuir who had a fleet of four vehicles in the 1960s, and operated a daily service to Brechin via Noranside, school services to Kilry and Achavan, a Saturday service to Alyth, private hire work for shooting parties and tours from Kirriemuir. ATS408 was a 29 seat coach with a Duple body when purchased new in August 1948, but had been fitted with service bus seats when I photographed it on 9th April 1966 near the village of Memus on the 4.15 pm return journey to Kirriemuir. It too is now preserved and restored to its original condition, being owned by Simpson and Smith of Killamarsh near Sheffield, who use it as a vintage bus for their "Cosy Coach Tours". It appears at rallies in their cream and brown livery.

Facing page upper: However, with the exception of the four Bedford OBs taken over in 1961, and two Bedford VAS with Duple service bodies new in 1962 and 1964, Northern only operated full size buses, even on quiet rural services, and the sub-depot (Rockwood Garage) at Methlick could accommodate four single deckers, although double deckers had to be parked outside overnight. By 1961, there was only one double decker required for the "commuter" runs from Cairnorrie via Udny Green, with two Albion Aberdonians and a "half cab" single decker for a school service to Ellon Academy. The Aberdonian had the lightest underfloor engine chassis available and was produced between 1957 and 1960. Of the 23 operated by Alexander, seventeen ended up running in the Northern region. While six of these had the coach style of Alexander body as seen on KCS425 (NNL12) when photographed on 8th July 1968, the remainder were of dual purpose design with a straight waistline, as fitted to KWG584 (NNL9) one of nineteen (NL3-21) new in 1958, of which FNL10-4 ran in Fife, and MNL18 was allocated to Larbert Depot in the southern region. KCS425, however, was new to Western SMT, as one of three KCS423-5 (I1384-6) purchased for evaluation in 1957, and transferred to Northern in November 1965 becoming NNL10-2. Despite being a very basic shed, Methlick Depot remained in use until 23rd April 1984 when the workings were transferred to Fyvie Depot.

The acquisition of Fyvie depot dated back to the purchase by Walter Alexander of George Cruickshank's Fyvie Bus Company in October 1931 with eight buses and the Aberdeen to Fyvie service. Situated midway between Aberdeen and Macduff, it supplied one front line vehicle for the through service, but was principally responsible for duplication and local services to Oldmeldrum, using elderly buses. It had an allocation of six buses between the 1950s and 70s, which in 1955 consisted of Coronation Coaches WG5501/30/9, 1934 vintage Leyland Lions WG2347-8 with their original bodies, and Leyland Tiger BWG528 new in 1949 on the Aberdeen to Elgin service. In May 1972, the depot became entirely OMO worked, and from January 1975 operated as a sub-depot of Aberdeen, still with a regular allocation, by now two 53 seat Fords, and four AEC Reliances. On 16th September 1976, SRS127 (NAC215) one of ten (SRS121-30)) 45 seat Reliances with 45 seat Alexander bodies to BET design new in September 1962, was photographed leaving the depot. This was the official stop for through services, and AC215 is about to depart at 3.25 for Inverurie to return with schoolchildren for Oldmeldrum. Withdrawn three years later, it was sold to a dealer in Carnoustie for scrap. Still inside the depot is AEC Reliance HMS246 (NAC97).

Although Northern had kept three buses overnight at Ballater in a shed at the Railway Station (and one in the garage at Castleton Place, Braemar originally built by the LNER) they only acquired the depot in Church Square with the takeover of Strachan's Deeside Omnibus Service in 1965. Prior to that, their Aberdeen to Braemar service (1) required three vehicles, one each from Aberdeen, Ballater and Braemar, with a registered circular school service (1A) from Ballater via Balmoral, and a school contract to Banchory. In 1958 there were still Leyland Tigers running on the Deeside services, with Coronation Coach WG5921 (P403) at Braemar and the former "Radio Coach" WG5928 (P410) at Ballater, but by 1961 these were replaced by Reliances with a Leyland Tiger WG8129 (NP550) on the Balmoral contract. After Strachan's was acquired, the Ballater allocation increased to seven vehicles, and by September 1973 the allocation was nine, made up of four Reliances, three Albion Vikings, one Ford and one Albion Aberdonian RSC427 (NNL23) photographed leaving the depot to take up the 2.00pm rail replacement 1C service to Banchory via Lumphanan on 25th September 1973. Exhibited at the Scottish Motor Show in 1957, it was fitted with tubular parcel racks and seats with head rests. It had operated for Scottish Omnibuses (S2) from June 1958 for a year before coming north. Withdrawn four months after this picture, it was converted to transport disabled children.

Facing page upper: Of the twelve vehicles taken over, only three had underfloor engines, two AEC Regal IVs (HD9304 and RMB158) and one AEC Reliance (SUG7), and all were acquired second hand. The last new vehicle bought was Foden GSA303 in 1951, and the final purchase was RMB158 (fleet number 6) in May 1963. It was new in July 1953 with a Plaxton Venturer 11 body, the revised front incorporating a large oval surround for the grille. One of three bought by Altrincham Coachways at a time of rapid vehicle turnover, it was sold to Sheffield United Tours (fleet number 229) six months later. Photographed on 23rd April 1965 reversing into the depot just before being absorbed into the Northern fleet, it has still to display its new fleet number NAB12. Withdrawn only three months later, it was sold to the dealer Dunsmore at Larkhall for scrap in November 1965.

Photographed on 28th November 1964 at Strachan's Aberdeen stance on Bon Accord Street, for the services to Braemar via Aboyne and Ballater via Ballogie on the South Deeside Road, were Fodens EYS222 (Fleet number 4) and FAV333 (number 27) awaiting outside the booking and parcel office to depart at 1pm. EYS222 was one of three Foden PVSC6s new to The Scottish Co-operative Wholesale Society Ltd of Glasgow in June 1947 with 32 seat Plaxton coach bodies. The SCWS had just taken over Campbell's Motor Services of Aberdeen the previous month, and continued to use the local name, as it did with other operators it acquired. In March 1957 it passed to Strachan's and was later converted for OMO operation with the sliding door controlled by a hydraulic linkage. Renumbered NF1 by Northern, it was withdrawn after a few weeks. FAV333 arrived new in July 1949 with a 35 seat service bus body constructed by Roberts, and had also been converted for OMO operation, but with a mechanical linkage to its folding door. It only remained in service with Northern renumbered NF4 until July, and like EYS222 was sold to Dunsmore of Larkhall for scrap in December 1965.

The Foden PVSC6 model with the 8.4 litre Gardner 6LW engine was a rugged machine ideally suited to the tortuous bends and steep inclines of roads in the Scottish Highlands, and all but the first two Fodens operated by Strachan's had this engine. From 1949, Foden's own two stroke engine was available, but JWU751 (fleet number 5) photographed near Cockbridge on 14th July 1965 while on a private hire, was fitted with a Gardner engine. It was new to Larratt Pepper & Sons Ltd in the South Yorkshire village of Thurnscoe in May 1950 with a Burlingham 33 seat coach body, passing to Strachan's in July 1959, but was never converted for OMO operation. Renumbered NF6 it was not withdrawn until September 1965 and also ended up with Dunsmore at Larkhall.

Facing page lower: Apart from the two members of the Strachan fleet which were painted into Northern fleet livery, the remaining ten buses were all sold to Dunsmore. As there was limited space at the Northern depot at Gairn Terrace in Aberdeen, a nearby piece of land adjacent to Whinhill Road was used to store buses awaiting disposal, and on 14th July 1965 most of the former Strachan fleet was parked there when I took this photograph. Foden GCA54 only displayed its Strachan fleet number 2 but not its Northern number NF5, as it had only run for Northern for a short while. It was the last Foden to be acquired by Strachan's, being new to the Welsh operator DC Jones of Ruabon in the county borough of Wrexham in September 1949. It had a rare Bellhouse Hartwell 33 seat coach body, and entered the Strachan fleet ten years later. Parked beside it is AEC Regal IV HD9304 with a 41 seat Plaxton Venturer body carrying fleet numbers 10 and NAB11 which was the first underfloor engined vehicle in the fleet. New to Broadhead of Dewsbury in January 1952, it passed through Mayne of Manchester and Harris of Cheadle to join the Strachan fleet in February 1961.

The solitary AEC Reliance in the Strachan fleet was SUG7, new to Wallace Arnold Tours Ltd in July 1953 with a 41 seat Duple coach body. Like the two Regal IVs it had a centre entrance and was not suitable for OMO operation. It was acquired in 4/63, given fleet number 9, but on entering the Northern fleet in May 1965 was sent for a major body overhaul, fitted with new seats and emerged in June with fleet number NAC51 allocated to Aberdeen Depot. Classified as a coach, it was used on private hires and was photographed on 2nd June 1966 in Inverness. However, much of the time it was used on ordinary service work, and although it could not display a route number, the destination box accommodated the standard destination screen. Surprisingly, it was transferred down to Blairgowrie Depot in September 1969 where it was used on school services and was withdrawn in December 1972, passing to a dealer in Hale who sold it on for scrap.

The only other bus in the Strachan fleet to be painted into Northern colours was fleet number 7, Leyland PS1 HOM776 which became NPA92 occupying a vacant number in Northern's fleet numbering system, although not quite accurate in relation to its chassis number or age. It was new in February 1948 with a rare 33 seat Santus body to Stockland Garage of Birmingham, and re-bodied with this Duple body in 1954. Interestingly, it has an oval grille on the front, a feature only available on Duple bodies built for the 1954 season. Acquired by Strachan's in May 1960, it was the last half cab bought and the only Leyland ever operated by the company. It passed to Northern five years later and was immediately repainted into fleet livery and transferred to Aberdeen Depot where it operated on a variety of rural services. It spent the last three months of its life at Buckie Depot, being withdrawn in December 1969 when it was sold to a dealer at Preston, ending up at Butlin's Holiday Camp at Pwllheli.

Facing page upper: By comparison, the Burnett fleet consisted entirely of AECs when taken over by Northern in January 1967, with only three of the ten single deckers being half cabs. Surprisingly, these were purchased in December 1963 when the seven Reliances were already in the fleet, and proved to be the last single deckers to enter service before the business was sold. They were acquired from the City of Oxford Motor Services at a time when their fleet consisted entirely of AECs, from a batch classified as AEC 9621A with 9.6 litre engines (OJO721-9) and were their last half cab single deckers. New in 1950, they were all sold in 1963 passing to other operators with OJO724/7-8 becoming Burnett 19-21. Although given Northern fleet numbers NA105/7, OJO724/8 were never painted into fleet colours, and delicensed in July 1968, being sold to a dealer in Comrie for scrap. The terminus for Burnett's services at Aberdeen was in Mealmarket Street, and I photographed OJO728 there on 30th May 1965, with AEC Reliance XSA620 in the background.

Of the seven AEC Reliances in the Burnett fleet, only two were bought new. There was a mixture of Plaxton and Burlingham bodies with a solitary Harrington example. Three had centre entrances, and one bought new with a Plaxton Highway body had service bus seats. As such, no two vehicles were the same, and parked at Mealmarket Street are fleet numbers 5 and 4, Plaxton Consort bodied WPT136 and Plaxton Venturer 11 bodied RWW545 with 41 coach seats and centre and front entrances respectively. They are waiting to depart for Stuartfield and Turriff at 9.50 am on 30th October 1966. The Consort model had a more stylish grille, and RWW545 had the later style of Venturer body with a front entrance ahead of the front axle and a glazed front dome. The former was new to Shaw Brothers of Byers Green in County Durham in 4/57, passing to Burnett in 4/62. It became NAC8 in the Northern fleet, and being allocated to the former Burnett depot at Turriff, came under the control of Macduff Depot, later moving to Peterhead and finally to Montrose Depot in June 1971. Delicensed by December 1972, it was sold to the contractor Binnie in Aberdeen in March 1973.

RWW545 by comparison, having a front entrance was converted for OMO operation in 1968, and remained in service until August 1975. Allocated to Macduff Depot with Northern, and given fleet number NAC5, it was one of only two Plaxton bodied Reliances at that depot and was normally used on local and school services. On 28th June 1968, I happened to spend the night at the picturesque fishing village of Gardenstown, where there was a bus parked overnight to take up the 8.10 service run into Banff in the morning. This arrangement only ceased when the driver retired in 1988, by which time he had a 49 seat Leyland Leopard with power steering. The village had grown up the cliff face, and the bus which parked at the top of the hill overnight descended down a steep and tortuous incline to the harbour in the morning to start its journey. The regular bus then was RWW545, photographed picking up children to take them to Banff Academy. By 1971 it had moved to Turriff Depot to operate a school contract from Cuminestown. New to Moseley of Barugh Green in May 1956, it came to Burnett's in March 1961 and was delicensed in August 1975, being sold to the dealer Muir in Kirkcaldy in May 1976.

Facing page upper: The other AEC Reliance with a Plaxton body at Macduff Depot was 3288WB (NAC141) photographed at the depot on 4th July 1974. Despite having its body rebuilt like NAC5, it was never converted for OMO operation, and was usually confined to school services. New to Sheffield United Tours (288) in May 1958 with a "Panorama Pioneer" body, it was sold to an operator on Skye Peter Carson of Dunvegan in July 1968, who ran a service from Glendale to Portree. In February 1970, he sold his company to MacBraynes which was in the process of being absorbed into the Highland Omnibuses fleet, and it passed with their Fort William operation to Highland in May 1970. However, it was not operated and instead joined the Northern fleet in September 1970, but did not enter service until April 1971, remaining at Macduff Depot until withdrawn in December 1975. It too was sold to Muir, later becoming a store shed near the village of Thornton, and finally returning to Muir's yard and scrapped in 1978. Parked beside it are 45 seat JMS49 (NAC98) new in 1956 which ran for 20 years, and 41 seat NMS361 (NAC150) new to Macduff Depot in 1960 for the premier Aberdeen to Elgin service and withdrawn in 1977. Although near the end of their lives, both still looked very smart.

Two of the ex Burnett AEC Reliances were never painted into Northern's yellow and cream livery, LSA600 with a Harrington body and GWH615 also with a centre entrance, but with a Burlingham Seagull body. Although given fleet numbers NAC4 and NAC3, they were withdrawn within a year. The other Reliance OAV146 was new to Burnett, and had a front entrance 41 seat Burlingham body entering service in June 1957. Allocated by Northern to Peterhead, it continued to operate out of Mintlaw which was its sub-depot, on its regular duty consisting of the 7.20 am 83 service from Stuartfield to Aberdeen via Mintlaw, returning at 5.20. Photographed in the late evening inside Peterhead's dingy depot on 6th July 1967, it remained allocated there until delicensed in May 1973. Its initial disposal was to Oakbank School in Aberdeen, but I next encountered it parked out of use at Newtonhill in a pale blue and cream livery. Later reported at Fordoun Flying Club, it was eventually acquired by the NE Bus Preservation Group in Aberdeen. Parked beside it is Albion Viking GRS343E (NNV43) which had arrived only three months previously.

Northern's use of the premises at Victoria Stables in Peterhead dated back to Alexander's acquisition of James Sutherland's business in March 1950, although the Sutherland family retained ownership, and continued to use it as a base for its goods haulage business. Most of the Sutherland fleet continued to run out of this depot, but two of the four post-war AEC Regals moved away almost immediately. New in 1947 as DSA113-6 (fleet numbers 107-10) they had rare dual purpose bodies built by Brush of Loughborough. This was to a similar design to Western SMT's AEC Regals, following their choice of this body to relaunch their Glasgow to London service after the war using Leyland Lion chassis. With 30 coach seats and sliding front doors they entered service with Northern as NA94-7, and NA95 was soon transferred to Aberdeen and 96 to Blairgowrie where they remained until withdrawn. NA94 was photographed at Peterhead Depot in Northern colours with a yellow roof in September 1964, and was withdrawn in December 1965 and sold to Dunsmore of Larkhall for scrap along with NA95 and 97.

Facing page upper: By contrast, NA96 at Blairgowrie Depot was painted into the more usual Northern livery for half cab single deckers with a cream roof and yellow window surrounds, which it retained until sold. Like the rest of the batch it had its sliding door replaced by a folding door, and was re-seated to 35 in March 1961 using second hand service bus seats. Although it was not possible to replace the somewhat restricted destination aperture, the screen fitted to NA96 was able to accommodate both the destination of Perth and the intermediate village of Guildtown, indicating that when photographed in September 1964 it was leaving Blairgowrie for Perth, and travelling directly by the A93 rather than via Coupar Angus. Remaining at Blairgowrie Depot until withdrawn in December 1965, it was surprisingly acquired by Scottish Omnibuses which was having one of its recurrent crises. Periodically short of buses, and as usual at Bathgate Depot, it was swiftly painted into Lothian green with the destination aperture painted over. It spent a year there with fleet number B46 using the common Scottish Bus Group practice of paper destination stickers. Thereafter, it was sold to the dealer Locke in Edinburgh, passing to a local contractor.

Facing page lower: Of the Sutherland fleet which was taken over by Alexander, only 26 of the double deckers survived to pass into Northern ownership, all fitted from new with platform doors. This feature was specified because of the harsh weather conditions in Buchan and in particular the blustery winds. They consisted of two all Leyland TD5s AV9962-3 (R663-4), ten Daimler CWA6 (RO681-90), twelve all Leyland PD1As RA 90-101 and two AEC Regents (RO692-3). The Leyland TD5s new in 1938 were unusual in having platform doors, and this rear view of R664 taken on 3rd October 1961 at Gairn Terrace in Aberdeen, just after withdrawal to become a seat store, shows the arrangement which resulted in the emergency exit being positioned on the front offside of the lower saloon. When new, it had the earlier style of rear upper deck, but as was customary, the body had been extensively rebuilt in the body shop at Aberdeen, fitting replacement window pans with sliding vents. Parked beside it and withdrawn at the same time are WG9180 and 9201 (R266/87) from the twelve Leyland TD7s transferred to Northern, with rebuilt front destination indicators. R287 passed on to a local contractor and R266 is now preserved at the Scottish Bus Museum at Lathalmond.

The AEC Regent IIIs model 9612E (FAV826-7) were fitted with curvaceous Massey bodies similar to those fitted to the last two Daimlers (RO689-90) and had been extensively rebuilt by the time this photograph of FAV827 was taken at Peterhead Depot on 14th September 1964. The curved windows at either end of the lower saloon had been replaced, and the front and rear domes rebuilt. New in September 1949 in Sutherland's livery of red, grey and cream, with fleet numbers 123-4, they were the last buses delivered before Alexander took over. Sutherland's order for twelve Leyland double deckers did not appear until the end of 1951 when all Leyland PD2/12s DMS340-51 entered service in Alexander's Southern area. Renumbered NRC21-2 almost immediately, they spent their entire lives at Peterhead, and with the more powerful 9.6 litre engine as compared with the Leyland 7.4 engine fitted to the Leylands they were popular with staff and passengers alike. NRC21 was withdrawn in May 1970 passing through the hands of Lancashire dealers to a Staffordshire operator for contract work around Sandyford Potteries. NRC22 remained in service until December 1970 when it was sold for preservation. Parked beside it is AEC Reliance OMS297 (NAC188).

It was not until January 1967 that more AEC double deckers came to Buchan when Burnett's were taken over, and four former City of Oxford Motor Services Regent IIIs (OFC377-8 and PWL412/5) joined the Northern fleet, becoming NRC23-6. OFC377-8 were new in May 1950 with 52 seat lowbridge Park Royal bodies becoming L153-4. They were acquired by Burnett's from a dealer in Macclesfield, and fitted with platform doors before entering service with fleet numbers 14-5 in February 1964. When taken over by Northern, they were operating out of Turriff and Mintlaw garages respectively thus coming under the control of Macduff and Peterhead depots. They subsequently moved around, running out of Elgin Depot from August 1970 until January 1971, finally ending up at Peterhead and Rosehearty respectively. They were both withdrawn in November 1971 and exported to the USA by the London dealer Omnibus Promotions, with OFC377 going to Chicago, and OFC378 ending up in Iowa. OFC378 was photographed at Mintlaw Depot on 27th May 1970 having arrived in from its school run from Ellon Academy to the village of Auchnagatt. Parked beside it is PWL412 soon to leave for the nearby picturesque village of Stuartfield for its return journey to Peterhead.

Facing page: Also parked down the side of the garage but further back, was PWL415 on Sunday 5th February 1967 just after the takeover, in a view which shows the old depot stores created from former railway carriages. It is not yet carrying its Northern fleet number, but retains its Burnett number 23 on the rear, its second as it was given number 16 on arrival. In a later version of the Burnett livery incorporating cream around the windows, it retained these colours until withdrawn in late 1969. Being of highbridge design, it was soon transferred to the former Simpson depot at Rosehearty and allocated to the Fraserburgh town service replacing the remaining former London Transport RT from the Simpson fleet HLW144, which was also highbridge and had platform doors. Sold to a dealer in Preston, although still languishing at Gairn Terrace Aberdeen in May 1970, it finally ended up in a Barnsley scrapyard at Royston.

AEC Regents PWL412 and 415 were new to City of Oxford Motor Services in December 1950 and January 1951 respectively with Weymann bodies similar in design to the London Transport RLH class, becoming L165 and H904. PWL412 had a 53 seat lowbridge body whereas 415 was to highbridge design seating 56. Sold to the dealer Transport (Passenger Equipments) Ltd in Macclesfield, they arrived at Mintlaw in December 1964 and December 1963 respectively and also had platform doors fitted. PWL412 (with fleet number 22) in the traditional version of the Burnett livery, was photographed on 30th May 1965 returning to the depot off service. As well as the Turriff based services, Burnett's operated from Mintlaw to the nearby village of Fetterangus, services through Mintlaw from Stuartfield to Aberdeen and Peterhead, from Maud to Aberdeen via Ellon, and from Old Deer to New Deer.

Facing page upper: PWL412 was photographed again on 27th May 1970 in Northern fleet livery as NRC25, leaving Peterhead on the 5.45 pm return journey to Stuartfield, after which it returned light to Mintlaw Depot. It remained allocated to Peterhead Depot operating out of Mintlaw outstation until withdrawn in January 1971 when it was replaced by a 67 seater Leyland PD3 NWG905 (NRB216). The other four buses regularly outstationed at Mintlaw at that time were OJO727 (NA106), OAV146 (NAC10), XSA620 (NAC145) and OSA800 (NAC144) all formerly in the Burnett fleet with an additional 45 seat AEC Reliance from the Peterhead allocation. PWL412 was sold in February 1971 to a dealer in Boston USA, acquired by a brewery on Rhode Island, and last seen in Connecticut.

Facing page lower: The Square, Mintlaw provided many bus connections, being the intersection of Northern's services from Fraserburgh to Aberdeen and Peterhead to Turriff, and situated just along the road from Mintlaw Academy. The depot provided vehicles for the more local services, and former Burnett AEC Reliance XSA620 worked out of the garage until delicensed in March 1978. As the last new vehicle bought by Burnett's, and the first for six years, it entered service in April 1963 with a 47 seat Plaxton Highway body with fleet number 7. On passing to Northern it was numbered NAC145 and was converted for OMO operation in 1970. Photographed on 4th July 1974 at 8.15 am, it has arrived from Stuartfield and is connecting with Ford WRS661L (NT61) on the 7.45 84 service from New Deer to Peterhead. In front is AEC Reliance FMS754 (NAC7) on the 7.15 75 service from Fraserburgh via St Combs which is connecting into the 7.31 72 service from Rosehearty to Aberdeen via New Aberdour operated by Ford VRG147L (NT47). XSA620 was finally sold for preservation in May 1980, and has now been returned to full Burnett livery by The Angus Transport Group.

Another ex Burnett AEC Reliance which continued to operate out of Mintlaw Depot was OSA800 (NAC144) which was photographed on 8th July 1968 at Aberdeen Bus Station, having arrived in on the 9.15 am 83 service from Stuartfield via Mintlaw. Parked beside it is one year old Albion Viking GRS338E (NNV38) which spent its entire fourteen year life at Aberdeen Depot, and eight year old AEC Reliance NMS362 (NAC151) from Macduff Depot which has arrived on the 7.35 05 service from Buckie, a route on which it had operated since new. It was transferred to Arbroath Depot in 1971 and sold in December 1976 for scrap. OSA800 was new in March 1958 to local coach operator McIntyre of Bucksburn with a 37 seat Plaxton Consort 11 body, passing to Burnett's in September 1962 and given fleet number 6. It was converted for OMO operation by Northern in 1972, and delicensed in March 1976, being sold to the dealer Muir of Kirkcaldy in May. However, it was not immediately scrapped and reappeared in 1979 bearing the name Banbeath Tours, a little-known operator from Leven, but was not broken up until 1981.

Before the Buchan services moved to the new bus station at Guild Street which opened in 1962, buses departed from Mealmarket Street where this photograph was taken on 3rd October 1961, five months after the Northern division of W. Alexander & Sons Ltd became a separate company. The yellow livery was not introduced until March 1962. Awaiting to depart are AEC Reliances NMS371 (NAC160) from Peterhead Depot on the 12.15 62 service to Peterhead via Ellon, and JWG709 (NAC129) from Rosehearty Depot on the 12.5 63 service to Peterhead via Cruden Bay. Both are 41 seaters in coach livery as are most of the vehicles on these services, although there are some AEC Reliances with 45 bus seats. However, only one double decker schedule still remains, and in the background is all Leyland PD1A DSA852 (NRA100) from Peterhead Depot, acquired with the Sutherland fleet, which has duplicated the 7.00 am 63 service from Peterhead awaiting to return on the 5.35 pm duplicate from Aberdeen. However, the requirement for duplication increased when the Aberdeen to Peterhead rail service ceased in May 1965 followed by the Fraserburgh line in October 1965. Also in the picture is Burnett's AEC Reliance OAV146 with a front entrance Burlingham Seagull body.

Facing page upper: While NMS371 left its parent depot for Blairgowrie in September 1969 and was withdrawn after seventeen years, JWG709 remained at Rosehearty Depot for its entire life of twenty years. New in June 1957, it was sold in December 1977, unusually for Northern, to Kelbie a dealer in Turriff, and later passed to Lawson of Kirriemuir. Now repainted into service bus livery and converted for OMO operation, it was photographed at New Pitsligo at 10 pm on 3rd July 1974 parked overnight for its daily schedule. As the service from New Pitsligo to Fraserburgh was now operated from Rosehearty, the New Pitsligo "sleeper" did the 6.45 am run into Fraserburgh and back before taking up the once a day 66 service to Peterhead via Strichen returning at 4.05 pm. On a Saturday, it did return trips to Peterhead at 1.30 pm for shoppers returning at 5 pm and a cinema run at 6.30 pm returning at 10.30 pm. First allocated to this duty in the winter of 1968 to provide a warm comfortable bus, JWG709 remained as the regular vehicle until replaced by an Albion Viking in 1975.

Northern preferred the AEC model rather than the Leyland Tiger Cub for its service bus fleet, and inherited twelve AEC Monocoaches and 100 AEC Reliances out of a total of 209 vehicles in the "AC" class delivered to the parent company, with the remainder staying in the southern region. Forty one Reliances had the dual purpose Alexander body, and 31 of these arrived in 1960 in two batches. The first 23 with NMS registration numbers (from the batch AC146-69) entered service in March and the final eight with OMS registration numbers (from the batch AC170-89) in June. Macduff Depot received NMS359-62 (NAC148-51) and NMS360 was photographed parked at the depot on 4th October 1961 having arrived in off the 3.30 pm 08 service from Aberdeen via Aberchirder. A similar picture could be taken today as Stagecoach continue to operate from the same premises, although the yard now has more protection from the elements.

Macduff Depot operated these four AEC Reliances on its front line services, the 08 service which required two vehicles and the 05 service from Aberdeen to Elgin via Banff to which it contributed three vehicles with the other intermediate depot, Fyvie, allocating one NMS366 (NAC155). Of the Macduff quartet, NMS361 remained at this depot for all its life being sold to Thomson, a dealer in Carnoustie in December 1977, passing on to a small operator George Hilldrup in the Essex village of Great Canfield. It was photographed on 7th March 1966 arriving at Cullen on a short working of the 05 service departing Elgin at 4.16 pm for Macduff. This route now operated as an hourly through service from Inverness to Aberdeen with a journey time of six hours. The other three at Macduff Depot all left in 1971, NMS359-60 for Aberdeen and NMS 362 for Arbroath. The first two returned in August 1975 for a final fourteen months, and NMS362 was delicensed in August 1976. They were sold to the dealer Muir in Kirkcaldy, but none were sold on to other operators.

The parent depot Aberdeen received three of the 1960 batch of dual purpose bodied AEC Reliances NMS376/508-9 (NAC164-6) and immediately allocated NMS376 to its outstation at Braemar where it was garaged overnight. From its remote outbase, it operated the 8.10 am 01 service into Aberdeen returning at 7.15 pm, with a run out to Lumphanan and back at 4.30 pm. Working out of Aberdeen Depot NMS509 did a double run out to Braemar and back, and both buses were out on a Sunday. Even after Northern acquired the Strachan business in May 1965 with the garage in Ballater, NMS376 continued to be the Braemar "sleeper" until finally replaced by a new Ford in September 1974, RRG560N (NT83). Being only a 45 seater with bus seats, this represented a deterioration in comfort, particularly when NMS376 had been the subject of modifications to further improve its heating system. This had resulted in changes to its front grille which was altered on two occasions, the second carried out in 1974, after which it was photographed on 14th May 1974 OMO operated, near Bridge of Gairn on the 6.10 pm 01 service from Aberdeen to Braemar. After fourteen years on the prestigious Deeside service, it was demoted to routine service work out of Aberdeen Depot, delicensed in September 1976 and sold to the dealer Muir in December.

Northern soon replaced the Strachan fleet and by the end of May, only three of the original fleet were still in daily operation, NAB11 on the Aberdeen via Ballogie service, NF3 at Braemar, and NF7 spare at Ballater. Also outstationed at Braemar were NMS376 (NAC164) on the Aberdeen service and SRS215 (NAC215) on a Banchory school contract. Ballater Depot housed NMS509 (NAC166), URS213 (NAC232) an AEC Reliance with an Alexander Y type body, on the Aberdeen/Braemar service, and KWG557/62 (NAC133/8). This pair were from the 1958 intake of Reliances with Alexander dual purpose bodies which had the earlier front grille and bumper arrangement than those entering service in 1960, as seen in this photograph of KWG562 arriving at Braemar and its terminus outside the Fife Arms Hotel. The destination screen is already set for its return journey to Aberdeen at 6.15 pm. Making up an allocation of seven buses at Ballater were two Leyland PS1s with Burlingham bodies CWG334-5 (NPA207-8) for local services .

Facing page upper: Strachan's Deeside Omnibus Service had three routes registered at the time it was bought by Northern: Aberdeen to Ballater via Maryculter and Aboyne, Aberdeen to Ballater via Ballogie, and Ballater to Braemar. Screened for Braemar displaying Strachan fleet number 8 is Foden LNW828, photographed on 23rd April 1965 opposite the depot, just before the takeover. New in March 1948 with a 33 seat Plaxton body, it was intended for Enterprise and Silver Dawn Motors of Scunthorpe, but was diverted to Mosby Tours of Kippax. Moving on to Travelways of Bradford in May 1952 it did not stay long, but was sold to Invicta Coaches of Leigh-On-Sea a year later, finally reaching Strachan's at the end of 1953, and was their first Foden acquired second hand. Much rebuilt, it had been converted for OMO operation with the sliding door controlled by a hydraulic linkage, and although given fleet number NF2 was withdrawn almost immediately. As with the rest of the Fodens, it was disposed of to Dunsmore of Larkhall in December 1965.

Facing page lower: Strachan's services were integrated into Northern's existing network, resulting in an enhancement of the through service from Aberdeen to Braemar via Aboyne (service 1), with a South Deeside service from Aberdeen to Ballater via Kirkton of Durris and Ballogie (service 1A). The latter, however consisted of only one return journey on weekdays with three on Saturdays. Foden FAV333 was photographed at Aboyne Bridge on 24th April 1965 on the Saturday only 12.00 service from Ballater to Aberdeen, a week before Northern took over. The ageing fleet consisted of nine half cab single deckers including seven obsolete Fodens, and three centre entrance underfloor engine AECs, the newest of which was eleven years old. This helped to create a perfect storm with the increasing use of private cars, a move away from holidays at home, and the impending closure of the railway to Ballater, which took place on 28th February 1966, thus leading to the sale of this long established family company.

As Ballater and Braemar were sub-depots of Aberdeen, only routine maintenance was carried out at Ballater, and there was no fixed paper allocation at that time. One significant movement was the return of AEC Reliance JWG690 (NAC110) to Braemar Depot to which it was allocated when new in July 1957, operating the Deeside service to Aberdeen until replaced by NMS376 three years later. It too remained in the area, only leaving Ballater Depot when delicensed in May 1977, acting as an unofficial Tow Wagon when required. JWG690 was one of the 70 AECs inherited from the parent company which had Alexander service bus bodies. The 1955 batch of 21were a mixture of Monocoaches and Reliances, but those delivered in 1956 were all Reliances with 45 bus seats and all were delivered new to the Northern area. By contrast, the 1957 intake JWG680-709 (NAC100-129) were fitted with 41 dual purpose seats, but again allocated to the Northern depots, and NAC104 was photographed still in coach colours at Elgin Bus Station on 7th March 1966 OMO operated, waiting to depart on the 3.30 short working to Nairn. New to Aberdeen Depot for the Elgin via Banff service, it was transferred to Elgin in November 1965, continuing to operate on the same route until moved to Arbroath in 1971.

Facing page upper: There was, however, one odd vehicle which passed to Northern, purely because it happened to be allocated to a northern area depot at the time.This was AEC Reliance FMS762 (NAC15), one of ten FMS758-67 (AC11-20) new in 1954 with Park Royal bodies. These were completed at Alexander's coach works at Drip Road Stirling where the 45 bus seats were fitted. The batch was split between Stepps Depot (AC11-4) and Grangemouth (AC15-20) for the Glasgow to Bo'ness route. FMS762 was transferred to Arbroath in 1958, along with two 45 seat Alexander bodied AECs from Perth Depot to replace three double deckers required at Montrose Depot. The only other AEC Reliance at Arbroath Depot at that time was JWG691 (NAC111) dedicated to the premier service from Aberdeen to Dundee. FMS762 remained at Arbroath Depot for the rest of its life, retaining its coach livery, and unlike the majority of the batch down south, kept its original front grille and trim. It was largely confined to the Arbroath Town Service to Brothock Bridge and Timbergreens on which it was photographed on 13th September 1964. Delicensed in June 1973, it was sold in September 1974 to a football club in Mintlaw. Interestingly, the other vehicles in this batch which passed to Midland were all withdrawn between 1969 and 1971, passing to dealers for scrap.

Below: After the split up of the Alexander empire in 1961, it was possible to see similar buses in the different liveries of the three constituent companies in bus stations such as Dundee, Perth and Stirling where this photograph was taken on 8th August 1965. Parked there were AEC Reliance NMS511 (NAC168) from Dundee Depot on the 19 service from Dundee to Glasgow, Midland's Leyland Tiger Cub MWG413 (MPD172) from Bannockburn Depot off the 38 service from Edinburgh, and Fife's Leyland Tiger Cub KMS493 (FPD124) from Dunfermline Depot off the 22C service from Dunfermline, all with Alexander dual purpose bodies. Beside them was Midland Daimler CVD6 BMS411 (MD16) with a Burlingham body from Milngavie Depot on a private hire. New in March 1948, it was now in service bus livery, and had only three months left before being withdrawn from service.

At Dundee Bus Station which was opened on 2nd June 1958, there were still Northern buses not yet painted into fleet livery when this photograph was taken on 24th October 1962. Still in the Alexander all blue service bus livery is AEC Monocoach GWG482 (NAC78) from Forfar Depot new in July 1955 with a 45 seat Alexander body in cream and blue livery, and soon to be repainted into Northern bus livery. Beside it is AEC Reliance JWG689 (NAC109) from Stonehaven Depot new in June 1957 already painted into Northern coach colours, but later also to be repainted into bus livery, and a third livery can be seen on JWG707 (NAC127) already in Northern bus livery. Also already repainted is DMS125 (NA99), the first of six AEC Regal IIIs (model 6821A with a crash gear box and 7'6" wide chassis) ordered by James Sutherland with Duple bodies and preselector gearboxes. These were not delivered until May 1951 when they appeared as A99-104 with 28'5" long 8' wide Alexander bodies with 35 coach seats, and were allocated to Grangemouth Depot for tours. Four of the Duple bodies were used to re-body ex SMT Leyland TS7s. Never popular with passengers or drivers, the AEC Regals were moved north in November 1957 to the former SMT depot in Dundee (code D2) at Westfield Avenue, and when it was closed in March 1959 were redistributed to Dundee (Seagate) NA99-101, Blairgowrie NA102, and Arbroath depots NA103-4 for local service work. NA99 survived until May 1972, being the last half cab single decker in service with the Scottish Bus Group.

Facing page upper: Lined up at Dundee Bus Station a year later on 24th August 1963, are half cab single deckers with a variety of liveries, all allocated to Dundee Depot where they remained until withdrawn. AEC Regal BMS468 (NA82) was one of eleven new between September 1947 and March 1948 with 35 seat Burlingham bus bodies with the emergency exit on the offside at the front. It has been repainted into the Northern livery for this class of vehicle which was usually confined to short distance service work. Leyland Tiger PS1 AWG544 (NPA9) is still in the all-blue Alexander livery used to replace the cream and blue colours in which all the post-war Alexander bodied Leyland Tigers were delivered, being regarded as dual purpose vehicles. When delivered it was allotted fleet number P750, but may never have carried it. Just out of the picture is AWG554 (NPA19) originally allotted number P760 and now in all yellow bus livery, another of the eight 1947 Tiger arrivals inherited by Northern. By contrast, BWG528 (NPA123) from the 1949 intake, with its cream roof, has already been re-painted into what was to become the standard livery for Alexander and Duple half cab bodies, although there were one or two exceptions such as CMS200 (NPA132) with a yellow roof. At the end is Leyland Tiger TS8 WG9327 (NP637) which retained its original body side trim.

There were 105 Leyland TS8 "specials" delivered to Alexander in 1939-40, and all but five were still in service in 1961. With fleet numbers P572-621 and P628-82, they seated 39 in dual purpose seats, and had proved reliable and versatile throughout the country, with 27 passing to Fife, twelve to Northern and the remainder staying in the southern region. Fife were still using them on front line services as late as 1957 with Anstruther Depot putting them out on the Leven to Newport service. Only eight survived until 1964, all with Midland, the last to be withdrawn being MP682 at Milngavie Depot on 30th September 1964. Northern inherited NP612-21/37/71 and the first to be withdrawn was NP671 at Forfar Depot in 1961. The remainder were all due to be taken out of service at the end of August 1963, which I was assured when I photographed NP615 from Rosehearty Depot at Fraserburgh bus station on 25th August 1963. Previously rebuilt in the body shop at Gairn Terrace with alteration of its side trim, and reglazing of the rear windows, it was the only one to receive fleet livery. It was sold with the others apart from NP616 to a dealer in Bellshill for scrap in December 1963, although Aberdeen's NP618 was still on the premises in February 1964.

Of greater interest that day was the unique 35 seat Pickering bodied Albion CX13 model CSA155 parked up at Rosehearty Depot. Fitted with a Leyland 8.6 litre engine by 1954, it had continued in service, despite being non-standard, until delicensed in February 1963. New in March 1946 to The Newburgh Bus Service of Ross and Cruickshank, it passed to James Sutherland in May 1949 (fleet number 28) with four pre-war Albion single deckers and a double decker (EAV161) with a rare Walker body fitted with a platform door. When acquired by Alexander in March 1950, CSA155 was given fleet number E37, and EAV161 became RO670 moving down to Cowdenbeath in March 1952 where it remained in service until June 1958. CSA155 was renumbered AL2 after being re-engined, and its body was given a major overhaul at Gairn Terrace with reglazing of its windows and modification of its destination indicator, but surprisingly it remained in coach colours initially with the "Bluebird" logo. However, it retained its radiator and Albion badge to the end, and was finally sold to the Bellshill and Mossend Scrap Metal Company of Bellshill in December 1963 and duly scrapped

Facing page upper: After the war, James Sutherland returned to specifying AEC Regals for his single decker fleet, although Leyland Tiger PS1s followed a year later with a return to Duple bodies. The unusual choice of body for this quartet, DSA113-6 (fleet number 107-10) was Brush of Loughborough, perhaps because of the ready availability of this particular design. When delivered, they had glass louvres over the side windows and the emergency exit was at the rear offside. Although initially operated in Sutherland colours after entering the Alexander fleet, they were later painted into this two tone blue livery incorporating the Bluebird fleet name in a cream flash below the windows. When photographed in Perth on a private hire, DSA115 (NA96) was operating out of Blairgowrie Depot, and had its glass louvres replaced with a continuous metal strip above the windows. The emergency exit had been moved to the front offside as carried out on DSA113-4, but not for some reason on DSA116. In addition the sliding front door had been replaced by a folding one, and it had been reseated in 1961. When repainted into Northern colours it was given a cream roof like DSA114 at Aberdeen Depot, whereas the two which remained at Peterhead Depot had yellow roofs.

Below: After a wartime allocation of Guy and Daimler double deckers, James Sutherland ordered all Leyland PD1As which arrived in two batches, DAV303-8 (fleet numbers 101-6) which arrived in May 1947, and DSA848-53 (111-6) in March 1948. Fitted with platform doors and 53 seats, they were comfortable, but with the smaller 7.4 litre engine lacked power, and the twelve similar vehicles ordered for 1950-51 were for the PD2/1 model with the more powerful 9.8 litre engine. Renumbered RA90-101 by Alexander, they were later reallocated and DSA853 (NRA101) was the only one to remain at its original depot of Rosehearty. It was photographed in Fraserburgh on 4th October 1961 returning from Peterhead on the 25 service, and shows signs of rebuilding at Gairn Terrace, with replacement of the half drop windows with sliding vents, reglazing of the front windows and modification of the destination screen with the addition of a route number aperture. Delicensed in September 1970, it was sold a month later to the dealer Gray at Braidwood.

Facing page upper: Almost twenty years later, and Leyland PD2/20 GCS230 (NRB169) is passing through Sandhaven on the 3.15 pm service from Fraserburgh to Rosehearty. Northern had an increased requirement for double deckers because of the development of the North Sea oil and gas industry. There had been no new double deckers since 1963, and ageing vehicles from the Simpson and Burnett fleets required replacement. It therefore acquired eighteen examples (NRB169-86) of this model from Western SMT in 1970 followed by thirteen more (NRB289-301) in 1971, with a mix of Northern Counties and Alexander bodies of which seven (NRB180-6) were to an earlier design. Surprisingly, none had platform doors, although Western were withdrawing identical vehicles with platform doors at the same time. GCS230-1/3-6 (NRB169-74) were new in 1955 with 55 seat Northern Counties bodies, and ran for fifteen years at Ardrossan (GCS230-1) and Johnstone (GCS233-6) depots on front line services. GCS230, formerly WSMT ND1144, was delicensed in November 1969, sent north to the body shop at Aberdeen for recertification and had just entered service when photographed on 27th May 1970. It moved down to Dundee in January 1972 and was withdrawn in August 1975, departing for Dunsmore's yard at Larkhall in December 1975 where it was scrapped.

Facing page lower:As the former Western SMT Leyland PD2s arrived in Buchan, the ex Simpson re-bodied PS1s were being withdrawn, the first two being in 1969. With fleet numbers NRA102-9 (HHE319-24 and KHE649-50) they had all remained at Northern's Rosehearty Depot, but only HHE320/2 and KHE650 were fitted with platform doors after arrival from Yorkshire Traction in 1965. The remainder were the first double deckers to be operated at Rosehearty Depot without doors, apart from a solitary PD1 (AWG365) RA27 from Alexander's own fleet which arrived in May 1952 and returned south to Milngavie in November 1955 after the arrival of 45 seat AEC Reliances. Only HHE320 and 323 were ever painted into Northern colours and survived two years longer, being withdrawn in 1971, and ending up on farms in Angus. All had their route number screens restored as they had been out of use when painted into Simpson's livery. HHE319 was the first to be withdrawn in October 1968 when it was sold to the Cranford School of Motoring, where it replaced a former Northern Leyland TD7 WG9631 (NR328). HHE324 was photographed in Fraserburgh on 30th October 1965, having entered service with Simpson in May 1965. It started off life in June 1947 registered AHE468 with a 34 seat Weymann body.

HHE323 (NRA106) was photographed at Fraserburgh Bus Station on 27th May 1970 awaiting its departure to Rosehearty. It now shows route numbers in its destination display, but is still screened 25 having arrived in from Peterhead, rather than 74 for its next journey. New to Yorkshire Traction in July 1947 and registered AHE467 with fleet number 736, it was re-bodied with a 59 seat highbridge Roe body in 1955 and re-registered before returning to service. It reached Simpson through the dealer North in Sherburn in Elmet, and was the last of the batch to be withdrawn in October 1971. Simpson had an intensive network of services in the North East when taken over in December 1966, including a circular town service in Fraserburgh, and routes to New Aberdour, Gardenstown, Rosehearty and Inverallochy as well as schools, works, tours and fishermen's services to Kinlochbervie. There were also services to Aberdeen from New Aberdour via Strichen, Udny Station and Kingseat Hospital.

Simpson also had a presence in Moray with an operation based on Forres after acquiring James Dean of Findhorn in March 1949. On a visit to the depot on 26th March 1966, the selection included OKP993, one of the shorter Leyland-Beadle rebuilds which entered service with Maidstone and District Motor Services in 1952 as a coach (CO265) with only 26 seats, incorporating units from Leyland TD5 FKO214. It passed to the contract operator Sowerby of Gilsland in 1960, moving north in 1962 together with OKP988 and 990. It alone survived to join the Northern fleet becoming NP838, but never received fleet livery and was delicensed in January 1967 and sold for scrap. Beside it is HHE321 and Duple bodied Bedford SB SSA474. Although given Northern fleet number NW268, it passed to Highland Omnibuses within six months and was converted for OMO operation. Ending up on Harris, it was withdrawn in November 1972, and moved on to run for James Peace on Orkney. At the front is Brush bodied Leyland Royal Tiger DHE343 converted for OMO operation. Acquired from Yorkshire Traction in October 1964, it became NPC62 with Northern, but was delicensed in July 1968 and sold for scrap without being repainted.

Facing page upper: Another Scottish company to buy Leyland Royal Tigers from Yorkshire Traction was Greyhound Coaches of Arbroath who bought four in June 1965, operating them from its base in Sheffield as well as Arbroath and Dundee. DHE338/45-6/51 were model PSU1/9 new in 1951 with 43 seat Brush bodies with fleet numbers 907/14-5/20. DHE345 initially operated in Sheffield coming north in June 1965, and was photographed on 14th July 1965 with fleet number 111 at the Greyhound Bus Station in Arbroath, having arrived OMO operated from the fishing village of Auchmithie. This was a service originally operated by Hunter and Nelson of Arbroath which was taken over by Greyhound in 1961 when Tom Alexander, who had founded the company in Sheffield back in 1949, wished to return to Scotland, and had already acquired a small company, McGibbon of Dundee, which operated a service to Fowlis and Muirhead. The Royal Tigers had a short life with Greyhound, with DHE346 delicensed within a few months and DHE351 sold to a contractor in Newcastle, but DHE345 was not withdrawn until July 1968.

Facing page lower: Also photographed on service to Auchmithie, on 11th July 1968 was FPN588C a Bedford J2 model new in 1965 with a 21 seat Willowbrook body to Ive of St Leonards in Dorset, coming to Greyhound in December 1967 from a small operator in Kent. It did not last long with Greyhound either and was withdrawn in early 1971 later entering preservation. Parked beside it is CCN167 (with fleet number 67) on the local service to Cliffburn Road, an all Leyland PD2/1 with a 58 seat highbridge body new to Gateshead and District in 1951. Transferred up from the Sheffield operation in May 1968, it was withdrawn from passenger service in July 1969 and demoted to providing transport for berry pickers. Other vehicles from the same batch also operated out of Greyhound's Arbroath Depot from time to time, but double deckers tended to have a short life with Greyhound, and the next fleet to arrive were similar vehicles from Plymouth Corporation, but from a 1953 intake.

Despite much of the operating territory of Northern being remote and rural, the policy was to only buy full size vehicles for service work, as continued to be the case for Fife and Midland as well. As an experiment each company purchased a single Bedford VAS with a 30 seat Duple Midland service body in 1962, and SRS134 (NW264) arrived in May allocated to Huntly Depot joining Bedford OB BWG42 on OMO operation. Now in Northern colours, it was photographed on 14th September 1964 near Fordyce on the 11.25 am service from Cullen to Huntly. Some time after Strachan's was taken over it moved to Ballater Depot for the school service to Crathie which was also OMO operated, but no use was found for it after that, and it was stored in 1971. In August 1972 it was sold to Carruthers of New Abbey who ran it for a further four years after which it was sold to a local building contractor in Dumfries. Northern did buy one further similar vehicle, ARG11B (NW265), in 1964 to replace the Bedford OB at Huntly, but it too was withdrawn in 1971.

While Northern continued to buy full size vehicles, lightweight buses began to appear in 1965 when the first Albion Vikings arrived followed by Fords from 1971. However, independent operators such as James Bean of Brechin often ran a varied mix of vehicles as seen photographed in his garage on 15th August 1965. HSR121 was one of two remaining FT39N model Albions used on the service run from Brechin to Forfar, and was new in May 1951 with a 31 seat Duple coach body. Behind it is 367CKA, a Foden PVRF6 model with a 2 stroke rear engine, preferred by coach operators to Gardner engines because of its performance. Although the chassis was built in 1951, it was retained for experimental work and was the last to leave the factory before it ceased bus production. It was given an early 41 seat Plaxton Panorama body with a unique rear end to accommodate the engine. and delivered to Toppings Super Coaches of Liverpool in April 1959, passing on to Bean in September 1964 and Collie who took over the business in May 1972.

Another unusual destination display can be seen on Leyland PD2/12 NDT997 which was photographed on 23rd June 1963 returning from its run on the Arbroath town service to Cliffburn Scheme. Unusually, it entered service as a "non PSV" vehicle with British Ropes of Doncaster for staff transport in 1953 with a rare body from local company Barnaby of Hull, and was the last body they built. Seating 59, it had features of various body builders of that era, perhaps through obtaining component parts from Metal Sections of Oldbury. One usual feature however was the placing of traffic indicators on the front wings. Delicensed in May 1967, it returned to service again, but was finally withdrawn the following year. Parked behind is a BMMO S9 model LHA363, one of two rare integral construction former Midland Red vehicles still running in Arbroath. New in April 1949 with a Brush body lengthened by Roe to seat 44, it had arrived in August 1962 with NHA580 a S10 model new in December 1949 with fleet number 3580 which was withdrawn in May 1964.

Facing page upper: There were a few Albions running for independent operators in Angus in the early 1960s, and Greyhound had two of the Valiant CX39N model with 33 seat Plaxton coach bodies which lasted until 1965. Both were new to Cotter of Glasgow in May 1950, a regular Plaxton customer, and HGE971 displays the roof-mounted horns. It passed to Hunter and Nelson of Arbroath, and on to Tom Alexander's Greyhound Coaches in 1961. They were used primarily for hires, schools and workers' services, and HGE971 was photographed on Marywell Brae in Kirriemuir on 11th September 1965. It was withdrawn in November 1965, but the other Albion HGE862 was already being scrapped by April.

Facing page lower:Greyhound Coaches also used double deckers on contract work, and Guy Arab 11 GRH193 with fleet number 108 was being used for transport to the Angus fruit farms when I photographed it beside the depot in Arbroath on 9th July 1968. New to East Yorkshire Motor Services (409) in December 1944 with a Roe highbridge body with a "Beverley Bar" roof, it was re-bodied in February 1953 by Roe to the same configuration. Sold to a dealer in June 1961, it arrived in Sheffield in January 1962 and was given fleet number 96, but moved north to Arbroath in August 1964 where it was fitted with the more powerful Gardner 6LW engine. Looking dilapidated, it still retains its destination panel proclaiming "Greyhound Sheffield," and was sold for preservation six months later. Parked behind it is SPT77, a Guy LUF new to Northern General Transport with fleet number 1677 in October 1955 with a 44 seat Weymann body. Converted for OMO operation, it came up from Sheffield in December 1977, one of six vehicles from this batch of 22 bought by Tom Alexander for his expanding company, both in Sheffield and in Scotland.

Facing page: The town service in Fraserburgh was operated by Simpson, and consisted of three circular routes from Broadgate taking in the bus station in Hanover Street. The regular vehicle allocated was former London Transport AEC Regent 111 HLW144, new in July 1947 as RT157 with a Park Royal 56 seat body. Together with HLW151, HLX227 and HLX237 (RT164, 410 and 419) it passed to Brown's Blue Coaches of Markfield who fitted platform doors before entering service in October 1958. It was sold to Simpson in March 1963 with the other three similarly rebuilt which were all withdrawn in 1965. HLW151 was broken up on site and HLX227 passed to the dealer North in Sherburn in Elmet and was also scrapped. HLW144 was photographed on service at Fraserburgh Bus Station on 30th October 1965, becoming Northern NRC1 after the takeover in December 1966, and continued in service until June 1968 without being repainted into fleet livery. It was sold in December 1968 to a dealer Hill in Comrie for scrap.

Northern had traditionally operated double deckers on its local network around Montrose, and historically had an allocation of six which increased up to nine in the mid 1960s. CMS366 (NRA63) was photographed parked in Montrose Square on 13th September 1964 on layover, having come in from Edzell on the 44 Circular Service. It was one of four Leyland PD1s CMS364-7 (RA61-4) delivered in August 1949 with 53 seat Alexander bodies to Leyland design. However, this batch had a new design of alloy window pan with flush glazing, and were the last PD1s delivered new to Alexander, although the chassis for CMS366-7 were actually intended for Western SMT. They spent all their lives in the north, allocated to Aberdeen Depot from new and underwent extensive body renovation in 1958. CMS367 remained there until transferred to Arbroath in July 1968 but Montrose Depot required additional double deckers for school services in 1963, and CMS364-6 came south, remaining until withdrawn in late 1970 with CMS366 continuing in service until December. All four were sold to a dealer in Braidwood for scrap. However, two of the previous batch which had been heavily rebuilt survived for a further month and were exported to the USA and repainted into London Transport red livery.

The final delivery of Leyland PD2s ordered by the parent Alexander company had the later style of Alexander body of four bay construction and came in two batches. DMS476/9-504 (RB118-44) in 1951, and DWG901-23 (RB145-67) in 1953. These were distributed throughout the three areas, with nineteen allocated to the southern region, sixteen to Fife and fifteen ended up with Northern. These also started life at Aberdeen Depot, with the exception of the last two DWG919-20 which went straight to Elgin, and DMS498/504 which were briefly at Stonehaven. DWG919 (NRB163) was photographed on 24th February 1970 arriving at Coleburn at 1.22 pm on a short working of the 35 service from Elgin to Aberlour. With dual purpose seats in the lower saloon and eight feet wide, there was a tolerable degree of comfort downstairs in these lowbridge bodies. It was the last of these 50 elegant vehicles to run in service, with all of the Fife and Midland ones withdrawn by 1971.However, the last two years of its life were eventful as it moved to Dundee in September 1972, was on loan to Central SMT in May 1973 moving on to Highland Omnibuses in September 1973. It returned to Dundee in April 1974 for a school contract, but was delicensed in May and sitting at Arbroath Depot in July as a source of spares. In December it was sold to a dealer in Hale, and eventually exported to Sweden.

This batch of Leyland PD2/12s had a long life at Aberdeen Depot on front line service work with the first not reallocated until 1968. When this photograph was taken at Aberdeen Bus Station on 12th February 1966, DMS487 (NRB127) had just come in from Echt on a short working of the 04 service from Tarland. It moved up to Elgin in January 1971, but was withdrawn in August and exported to Boston, Massachusetts. Parked beside it is Leyland PD3/3 NWG896 (NRB207) new in 1960 with a 67 seat Alexander body, and one of 20 from the similar 77 delivered to Alexander in 1958 and 1960 to join the Northern fleet, with the remainder becoming Midland vehicles. There had been no further deliveries of new double deckers to this region since 1953. It moved to Dundee in April 1976 to help with a recurrent shortage of vehicles, and was sold for scrap in November. By contrast, RRS595 (NRB285) was one of a batch of seven, RRS590-5/7 (NRB280-6) delivered three months after Northern was formed, with local registration numbers, and the "St Helens" style of new look front. However, they still appeared in blue with no signs of new ownership, as it was March 1962 before the yellow and cream colours appeared. It operated at Aberdeen all is life, and was the first of the batch to be withdrawn in 1977. Scrapped like the remainder, these half cab vehicles were by then obsolete in an era of rear engine vehicles.

Nearly ten years later, the scene at Dundee Bus Station on 31st July 1975 is of twenty year old Leyland PD2s originally transferred from Western SMT. These were to provide increased capacity for oil industry developments and the replacement of elderly vehicles acquired from Burnett's and Simpson's, but were now needed for increased contract and school work. GCS235 (NRB173) entered service in 1970, but allocated to Arbroath, moving to Dundee in September 1974 and withdrawn for scrap two years later. HCS986 (NRB177) was from Western's 1976 intake of Leyland PD2/20s with the revised triangular destination display, and increased seating of 59. HCS984-8 became NRB175-9 on transfer and were allocated across the company, but HCS986 went to Dundee where it stayed until delicensed a month after this picture was taken. It ended up as a caravan at Skegness. RMS734 (NAC200) is interesting, because although it arrived in May 1961 as part of Alexander's order for AEC Reliances (RMS724-43), it wasn't licensed until June after Northern was formed, and therefore entered service with Northern at Elgin. The remainder of the batch were allocated to Midland depots but were all withdrawn by 1975. Transferred to Stonehaven Depot in December 1972, it is down from Aberdeen on the 11 service via the coast. It survived until 1977.

Facing page upper: Four years later in September 1979, and the scene at Dundee Bus Station is very different with the unusual sight of Bristol Lodekkas, the first and only batch operated by Northern. With the perennial requirement for double deckers for school contracts, five FLF6Gs were acquired from Midland in May 1979, having originally been part of the SBG/NBC Bristol VRT/FLF exchange. RVW391/3-4D, RWC943D and UEV221E were new as Eastern National 2865/7-8/71/83 becoming Midland MRD195/7-8/201/9 and finally Northern NRD1-5. The initial allocation was NRD1 at Aberdeen, 4 at Montrose, 3/5 at Dundee and 2 at Elgin. The first two only lasted a year. NRD 3 and 5 moved up to Elgin to join NRD2 for Lossiemouth High School contracts, and the last to be withdrawn was NRD2 on 30th November 1983 becoming a Driver Trainer. When photographed, NRD3 and 5 with its advert for "Express Jet" were parked up beside Fife Leyland Leopard FPE133 and Northern Ford NT151 from Montrose Depot down on the 11 service from Aberdeen, both with Duple Dominant bodies.

Facing page lower: Northern bought a couple of Albion Lowlanders SRS111-2 (NRE1-2) in 1963 to evaluate them, running them on the frequent busy service from Aberdeen to Inverurie alongside the 1961 batch of Leyland PD3s. They proved to be the last new double deckers to be delivered for sixteen years, when Daimler Fleetlines ASA21-8T arrived. They arrived in April in different liveries with SRS 111 in what had become standard livery apart from maroon mudguards. However, there had been experiments with the double decker livery as well, and SRS112 was given a cream roof with maroon mudguards. It was photographed at Aberdeen Bus Station on 26th August 1963 waiting to depart on the 12.05 service to Inverurie. They remained at Aberdeen Depot until December 1971 when they moved north to Elgin in exchange for a pair of PD3s KWG654/9 (NRB193/8) as they could seat four more passengers. Only six more Lowlanders were operated (NRE3-8) coming from Western SMT in 1976, with UCS646 from the 1963 batch and VCS414/7/9-20/2 the 1964 arrivals. They were, however, all sold for scrap two years later.

Northern's own two Lowlanders, which were their first vehicles with semi-automatic gear boxes, remained at Elgin Depot until January 1978 when they moved to Dundee for the last ten months of their lives, after which they were sold to a dealer in Carnoustie and scrapped. Joined by Western VCS419 they were used on school contracts from Elgin and Forres depots, with SRS112 at Forres until 1976. Now in standard fleet livery, they were photographed at Elgin Depot on 30th July 1975 during the school holidays. Parked beside them are ex Western SMT Leyland PD2/20s HCS987 (NRB178) and HSD13 (NRB185) new in 1956 with bodies by Northern Counties (similar to HCS986 on page 52) and Alexander respectively. HCS987 first entered service at Aberdeen in April 1971 moving to Elgin in October 1973, and only had another month in service before being withdrawn. HSD13 was one of the batch HSD8-14 (NRB180-6) with a more upright front profile which were all allocated to Western's Kilmarnock Depot when new. It came immediately to Elgin in October 1970 after being overhauled in Northern's body shop and was also withdrawn in August 1975. Both were sold to dealers for scrap.

Facing page upper: Ten years earlier at Elgin Depot on 11th February 1966, and an equally smart line up of single deckers. The Alexander bodied AEC Regals had metal framed bodies with many surviving for twenty years remaining at the same depot for much of their lives. The last to be withdrawn at Elgin Depot and seen in this photograph was AWG633 (NA46) new in August 1947 and not delicensed until July 1968. As a tribute to the indestructibility of its body, it was surviving as a builder's hut at Westhill in 1976. The first Alexander body to this design actually entered service on 12th July 1946 on AMS503 (NA28) also at Elgin Depot, but AMS498 (NA23) also in this picture was licensed three months later. It was delicensed in 1967 and ended up as a mobile shop in Aberdeen. The line-up is completed by Leyland PS1 EAV461 (NPA200) new to James Sutherland in March 1948 with a 35 seat Duple coach body. The only one of the six acquired by Northern to come to Elgin Depot, it moved east to Buckie in 1966 and had a long life being the last of the batch to be delicensed, and was not sold until May 1970. It then passed through the hands of two dealers before ending its days in one of the Carlton scrapyards.

The Alexander body on Leyland PS1 BWG528 (NPA123) photographed at Dundee Bus Station in February 1966 was of composite construction, but had also been extensively rebuilt and therefore survived for 21 years. Interestingly, the chassis of Leyland OPS2/1 DMS815 (NPB2) parked beside it also originally had a similar body, from BWG517 (PA112) which had operated in the southern region at Stepps Depot, but its body was beyond economical repair and scrapped in 1961. When the original 8' wide chassis of DMS815 was used in the construction of double decker Leyland PD3/3C RMS682 (RB250), it resulted in its 8' wide Alexander body being mounted on the replacement 7'6" wide chassis which had come from BWG517. This front view also provides an interesting comparison with AEC Regal DMS127 (NA101) next in the line up, which also has a 1951 8' wide Alexander body on a 7'6" wide chassis, but only because of a change of body builder after Sutherland's order was changed by Northern. DMS815 was withdrawn in 1969 and scrapped, but DMS127 survived until April 1971, was sold to a contractor in Fochabers, and later entered preservation.

The batch of six AEC Regals ordered by Sutherland were intended to have Duple bodies similar to that on EAV636 (NPA201) photographed at Northern's headquarters in Gairn Terrace, Aberdeen on 12th February 1966. However, when the order was changed to Alexander bodies, four of the Duple order were used to re-body 1937 Leyland TS7s. EAV636 was one of six Leyland PS1s EAV458-61/636 and ESA205 (NPA197-202) delivered over a year starting in March 1948, and withdrawn in 1969-70. They were Sutherland's last new single deckers having 35 seat dual purpose bodies and sliding doors. Although as was routine they were extensively rebuilt in the body shop at Aberdeen replacing half drop windows with sliding vents, they never received folding doors, and were never converted for OMO operation. As such, they were principally used for short distance services and school work, and EAV636 was being used in this manner at Fyvie Depot from 1962 onwards, having moved down from Rosehearty Depot. It was delicensed in September 1969, and sold to a contractor in Airdrie, not being scrapped until 1976.

Another 8' wide body on a 7'6" chassis, this time a Duple body but again on a Leyland PS1 chassis, was that on FDK908 of Mitchell of Luthermuir, photographed at their depot on 11th September 1965, two years before the company was taken over by Northern. It was new to Yelloway Motor Services Ltd of Rochdale in August 1947 with a 33 seat Burlingham body, and was acquired by Mitchell in 1956. Five years later, it was fitted with a 31 seat Duple coach body new in 1950. This came from Ribble Motor Services of Preston which had re-bodied a Leyland TS7 TRN7768 new in 1936 also with a Duple body, extending its life by ten years. Mitchell acquired the vehicle through the dealer Millburn Motors of Preston, but scrapped the chassis, and operated the re-bodied FDK908 until January 1967 when it was sold to a Boys Brigade Company in Glasgow. Behind in the garage is another Leyland PS1/1 JC9033, this time with a Burlingham body, with which it was new to Williams of Portmadoc in March 1948, reaching Mitchell via other operators in 1960, and was only withdrawn just before the takeover.

Like so many independents, Mitchell had a very varied fleet with some acquisitions being single purchases from dealers. Such a vehicle was NKT966 photographed leaving Strathcathro Hospital on 11th September 1965 on a contract service. One of Maidstone and District's semi-chassisless rebuilds by Beadle of Dartford, it incorporated the running units of AEC Regent CKE466 (DH332) integrated with a new full-fronted body. Entering service in January 1952 as a 35 seat coach with fleet number CO238, it was rebuilt as a 39 seat service bus with a single destination indicator in 1955 and renumbered SO107. Withdrawn in 1960, it reached Mitchell via the dealer Fleet Car in Dunchurch, entering service in February 1961 without modification, retaining its sliding door and bus seats. As such it was mainly used on school and contract work, being withdrawn six year later and sold to the dealer Tiger of Salsburgh for scrap.

Another comparatively rare vehicle in the Mitchell fleet was Brockhouse bodied Maudslay Marathon 111 XS6708 photographed on service from Brechin to Luthermuir on 11th September 1965. It started off life in the fleet of Young's Bus Service of Paisley new in November 1949 as one of ten coaches, XS6658-63 and 6705-8 (M2189-98) with 33 high back seats and sliding doors, of which only the first two did not have full fronts. However, they had a short life in this role, and when Western SMT took over Young's in January 1951, they were painted into their black and white coach livery. XS6663 and 6705-8 were used on the Glasgow to London service for a few months, and then joined the coach fleet at Johnstone. They moved over to the Isle of Bute in May 1958 for tours and service work repainted into dual purpose cream and red livery, and were delicensed in September 1960. XS6708 entered service at Luthermuir in December 1960 running until April 1966 and was sold to the dealer Millburn Motors in Glasgow and scrapped.

Facing page upper: Of the eleven vehicles in Mitchell's fleet taken over by Northern on 1st October 1967, four never received fleet livery but were given fleet numbers and remained in service for some time, even being relicensed for periods. A Guy LUF SPT69 (NGA1) from the same batch operated by Greyhound was finally withdrawn in mid 1969. Two Bristol LWL6Bs JYG740/8 (NE2-3) with Eastern Coach Works "Queen Mary" bodies new to West Yorkshire (final fleet numbers SBW5/11) survived until late 1968. However, similar LTA961 (NE1) photographed at the depot on 1st June 1969 continued in service until February 1970 and was sold in October to a dealer in Comrie for scrap. Similar to the West Yorkshire Bristols, it was also new in 1951, to the Southern National Omnibus Company of Exeter (1327), the chassis classification denoting a 30' long 8' wide version with a Bristol engine. It was acquired by Mitchell in March 1966 via the dealer Norths of Sherburn-in-Elmet and proved to be a versatile and reliable vehicle.

Facing page lower: Further variety in the Mitchell fleet was provided by another Maudslay Marathon 111, this time with a complete full front, and no immediately identifiable radiator features. Plaxton bodied BTS187 was new in October 1949 to Watson of Dundee with a 33 seat coach body for their tours fleet and they subsequently modernised it by returning it to the body builders to have a full front fitted. It was sold to Comfort Coaches of Dunfermline by February 1959 and on to Hogg of Carlisle in March 1963, coming to Luthermuir in May 1966. It had a relatively short life with Mitchell's and was withdrawn three years later, ending up as a showman's vehicle. With the widely used AEC 7.7 litre engine and dual purpose seats, it was a useful and comfortable vehicle, and its destination screen was discreetly incorporated above the windscreen. At the time of the takeover, Mitchell had a network of services from Luthermuir to Brechin and Montrose, Brechin to Strathcathro Hospital, Brechin Town Service, Montrose to Strathcathro Hospital, Montrose to Craigo and Montrose to Inverbervie, but within five years this had been simplified and Luthermuir was only connected to local networks through occasional journeys to Brechin via Strathcathro, and three runs a day to Montrose.

The 33 seat Plaxton coach body with a manually operated sliding door, was very popular with many bus operators in the early post-war period, as there was no trace of austerity in its design because Plaxton had not been involved in body construction during the war, and the seats fitted were up to the best standards of 1939 – before wartime restrictions occurred. Such an operator was Hay of Elgin, who kept a fleet of half a dozen vehicles in the early 60s, operating from Elgin to Forres via Dallas, Elgin to Pluscarden and from Aberchirder to Banff, Keith and Huntly. Photographed at the depot in Elgin on 26th March 1966 was an example of the 1948 variant of the body with a single-panel driver's screen, but also showing the chromium-plated pillars between all the main side windows to good effect. This resulted in a very elegant profile as seen on Leyland PS1/1 SO9035 new to the operator in November 1949, and now used on the Forres service. Parked in front of the garage and used exclusively for tours, is Bedford SB8 LCS806 new to Garnock Valley Motors of Kilbirnie in March 1958 with a 41 seat Plaxton consort 11 body.

Nearby in Forres at Simpson's depot, photographed on 5th February 1967 are the two Leyland Royal Tigers model PSU1/13 bus version, with the rather austere, box like 44 seat Leyland body designed for this model. With power operated doors from new, they were already converted for OMO operation when acquired from Ribble in September 1963 via the dealer Cowley in Salford. ECK561 (fleet number 298) was the first of the batch of 120 to enter service with Ribble in December 1951 becoming NPC68 with Northern in December 1966. It was delicensed in April 1967, but relicensed later in the year and finally sold for scrap in February 1969. ECK616 (353) which latterly operated OMO out of Penrith Depot, became NPC69 and operated until July 1968. Like DHE343 (NPC62) in the corner it retained the all-green livery. Parked in between is the first official replacement from the Northern fleet, Leyland PS1 CWG287 (NPA185) with a metal framed Alexander body, allocated from Elgin to Forres Sub-depot to replace the Beadle rebuild OKP993. It had come up to Elgin Depot from Stirling in August 1955 remaining until withdrawn in March 1971, sold to a contractor in Aberdeen and finally scrapped in October 1975 when 25 years old.

Facing page upper: In addition to these three Leyland Royal Tigers, another five passed to Northern, all from a batch new to Rhondda Transport of Porth in May 1952 with 44 seat Weymann bodies. LNY358/64-7 (fleet numbers 317/23-6) were acquired via the dealer Norths of Sherburn in Elmet in August 1964, along with LNY362 which however returned south in April 1965. Northern allocated them fleet numbers NPC67/3-6 respectively, but converted for OMO operation, they all remained in Simpson's colours in the green and cream livery at Rosehearty Depot, and were all withdrawn during 1968. LNY358 was assessed by Highland Omnibuses in February 1967, but returned and sold to a dealer in Coatbridge in August 1968. The remainder passed to a dealer in Comrie for scrap, but LNY 367 photographed at Rosehearty on 5th February 1967 I later saw with a showman in Glasgow in March 1969. The other Leyland Royal Tigers which were at Forres came under the control of Northern's Elgin Depot, the initial allocation at Forres Sub-depot in December 1966 being DHE343, ECK561/616, OKP993 and HHE321, KHE649 and three Ford coaches. This size of fleet was required for services to Dyke, Findhorn, RAF Kinloss, Forres town service and school and works contracts.

Facing page lower: Northern's NPA class of Leyland Tiger PS1s outlived the Midland MPA and Fife FPA vehicles, the last one of the 216 operated by the Alexander companies being BWG529 (NPA124) at Buckie Depot, which was delicensed in August 1971 when 22 years old. Although its Alexander body was of composite construction, BWG326 (NPA100) had been rebuilt in Northern's body shop, and was fifteen years old when photographed at Forfar Depot on 24th August 1963. However, it still retained its original plywood coach seats with tartan moquette, and there was little evidence of window re-glazing. Of the 195 PS1s with Alexander bodies, PA61-160 had composite bodies and PA76-125 had these coach seats which made them suitable for tours and private hires. PA1-59 (there was no PA60) had metal framed bodies, and this construction was resumed from PA161 until the final Alexander bodied one PA196. BWG326 was new in September 1948 and moved up to Forfar from Larbert Depot in April 1955 remaining until delicensed in May 1970 when it was parked up at the depot. It later passed to Telefilms, a dealer in Preston.

Northern also acquired Weymann bodied Leylands from Mitchell of Luthermuir, but Tiger Cubs (model PSUC1/1) JBO89/96 which were given fleet numbers NPD13-4 and repainted into fleet livery. New to Western Welsh of Cardiff in 1954 with fleet numbers 1089/96, they were acquired through the dealer Norths of Sherburn in Elmet in October 1966. JBO89 was licensed in December 1966, but JBO96 did not enter service until after Northern took over in October 1967. Both were converted for OMO operation early in 1968, and like the rest of the Mitchell fleet operated out of Northern's Montrose Depot where this photograph was taken on 9th July 1968 of JBO89, which had acquired a small front grille. One bus however continued to be outstationed at Luthermuir for the Brechin service. Both were due for withdrawal in January 1972, but JBO89 was finally delicensed in October 1972, both going to a dealer in Hale and scrapped. Also parked is AEC Reliance JWG697, new in April 1957 to Montrose Depot for the Aberdeen to Dundee service, and remaining there all its life until December 1975 when it was transferred to Macduff for three months before sale to Muir in Kirkcaldy for scrap.

Facing page upper: The third Leyland Tiger Cub in the Mitchell fleet (LVD263) came from a stock order for the dealer Millburn Motors of Glasgow, which followed on from Alexander's own order for 40 of the PSUC1/2T model with the recently-introduced Alexander coach body. The pair (LVD262-3) were new in October 1954 as 41 seat coaches, but first registered to Hutchison of Overtown in May 1955, and like many new vehicles in this fleet were soon sold on. LVD262 went first in February 1958 to Murray & Sons in Stranraer, and eventually ended up with McLennan of Spittalfield for spares. LVD263 was sold back to Millburn Motors who fitted 45 service bus seats and sold it to Gibson of Moffat in November 1957. Returning again to Millburn Motors, it next passed to Mitchell in April 1967, and became Northern NPD15 on take over. It fitted in well with Northern's own fleet, and was painted into the "reverse" livery, converted back to 41 seats out of an Alexander bodied AEC Regal and fitted for OMO operation. It operated from Montrose Depot where it was photographed on 11th July 1968, moved south to Dundee in December 1969 and was sold along with NPD13.

Northern inherited eight of Alexander's fleet of Leyland Tiger Cub coaches (PD1-40) new in 1954, the remainder staying in the southern region joining the Midland fleet. NPD3-12 (FMS720-9) had all come north in March 1955, NPD3-6 to Dundee Depot and NPD7-12 to Aberdeen. They remained at their respective depots until the last few months of their lives, when NPD8 moved to Dundee and NPD11 to Arbroath. All were withdrawn in 1972, whereas the Midland vehicles were all off the road by the end of 1971. Northern initially applied their new colours to the original coach livery, but NPD7-8 later appeared in a reverse livery as seen in this photograph of NPD7 and 10 at Elgin Depot on 26th March 1966. Initially intended for long distance services, they were never converted for OMO operation, acquired roof quarter lights and retained their one piece destination screens and manually-operated doors. Parked behind are CWG331-2 (NPA204-5) Leyland PS1s with Burlingham "sunsaloon" bodies converted for OMO operation.

The Alexander coach fleet was transformed with the arrival of the first underfloor engine "Coronation" coach in 1952, with a centre entrance 41 seat Alexander body on a Leyland Royal Tiger PSU1/15 chassis. Of the 74 (PC1-27/38-84) eleven passed to Northern, NPC1-6/25 and 55-7/61, of which the last four were new in 1953 with a revised design with a broad mid-panel band. NPC61 in fact received a second body in April 1954 after the original was burnt out in a fire. They were all withdrawn by 1972, the last in service being NPC57 at Rosehearty in August 1972. NPC56 photographed at Aberdeen Bus Station in July 1967 had been converted to front entrance for OMO operation in January 1967 followed by NPC1, but they continued to operate the Aberdeen to Glasgow service, and like NPC57 which was also converted in July 1968 never operated as such. However, the conversion proved too expensive, and although Fife similarly altered FPC50/2-3 with livery variations, and Midland MPC17/47, only MPC17 did operate OMO, while at Oban Depot. NPC56 still retains its original seats and split destination screen, and now has glazed cove panels and tubular parcel racks, but has lost its front visor. Parked beside it is Albion Viking GRG425E (NNV25) down on service from Fraserburgh, with an unclear (R) depot code, and incorrect (reversed) route number.

Facing page lower: The original Alexander "Coronation Coach" had been conceived for the 1937 Coronation, and was as sensational in its day as its successor in 1953. The first WG5487 (P351) appeared in the cream and blue livery with the main side flash red with a crown emblem, a variation which was repeated in 1953 when some of the second batch of Royal Tigers with broad mid-panel bands were similarly treated. With a rear luggage locker, a Clayton heater and the emergency exit opposite the entrance ensuring the maximum capacity of 35 seats, they were ideal for long distance services, and were still used on such until the 1950s. Aberdeen Depot still had a fleet of fourteen in 1957, and although twenty years old were still running them on Deeside and Donside services. WG5514 (NP375) was photographed on 3rd October 1961 four months after the formation of Northern, but still shows no external evidence of it. It has been rebuilt with sliding vents, having had the original sliding door replaced before the war, and retains its side sweeps. It has lost the illuminated "Bluebird" panel and glass louvres over the side windows which have been replaced by a continuous rain strip. It was parked in Aberdeen, having come in from Keig via Alford and Kemnay, and was due to return to its home depot of Alford at 6.15 pm. It was finally delicensed on 30th September 1962 and sold to a dealer in Aberdeen in February 1963.

Above: The "missing" Leyland Royal Tigers (PC28-37) with 41 seat centre entrance Leyland coach bodies were part of a cancelled order by George Rodger, a Motherwell haulage contractor who had intended to start up express bus services. They entered service in May 1952 split between Fife's Kirkcaldy Depot (FPC29/34-7) and Aberdeen (NPC28/30-3). Northern's allocation never changed over the years except that NPC33 moved to Rosehearty in September 1969 and was the last to be withdrawn in February 1972, the remainder being taken out of service after the 1971 tourist season ended. They led a very uneventful life, remained in coach livery and with no significant body alterations were latterly kept for private hires and school work. NPC30 was photographed at Aberdeen Bus Station on such duties on 8th July 1968 showing the semaphore indicators and the unusual arrangement with the destination in the nearside box. The Fife allocation, however, had a much more varied life with FPC29 and 37 converted to front entrance with a contemporary Alexander front for OMO operation for which they were used with livery variations. FPC35 however also acquired a new Alexander front after an accident, but retained its centre entrance and was thereafter confined to contract work. They were all withdrawn in 1970.

The next dual purpose coaches delivered to Alexander were the 50 Alexander bodied Leyland TS8s WG8101-50 (P522-71) in 1939 of which four passed to Northern, and NP532 (later photographed delicensed in Macduff Depot-see page 4) was photographed on 4th October 1961 opposite the depot on the local service from Macduff to Banff/Whitehills on which it was the regular allocation. Of the other three, NP533 was at Dundee Depot and NP550/64 at Aberdeen, but only NP564 was repainted into yellow and cream. It had the standard Northern single deck livery with a cream roof and cream side flashes whereas NP550 like 532 had been rebuilt with removal of the side flashes and was blue all over. Like NP532 they had all been at their respective depots since the early 50s, and were delicensed by August 1963 and sold to the Bellshill and Mossend Scrap Metal Company. The Aberdeen pair were in daily service until withdrawn, with one, usually NP550, latterly at Ballater Depot for the Balmoral contract.

Facing page lower: Northern acquired a depot on Markethill Road in Turriff with the operation of Burnett of Mintlaw in January 1967, and placed it under the control of Macduff Depot. The allocation of four vehicles remained constant until reduced to three by March 1982 after the initial "Scotmap" review of transport facilities and sustainable bus services. This was further reduced a year later after a local Banff "Scotmap" exercise, leaving one bus, by then a 53 seat Alexander bodied Ford, with USO184S (NT184) alternating with USO185S (NT185). Leyland National MSO15W (NPN15) was the intended bus which was required to work the local circular service via New Byth, but the outstation was closed on 23rd April 1984 and the work transferred to the parent depot which surprisingly allocated a Leyland Leopard with a 49 seat dual purpose Duple body, CRS70T (NPE70). A visit on 8th July 1968 showed the absence of any former Burnett buses, but three AEC Reliances, and inside the garage a former Sutherland Duple bodied Leyland PS1 ESA205 (NPA202) on loan from Stonehaven Depot for a school contract from Cuminestown to Turriff Academy. Sitting outside is NMS359 (NAC148) which has arrived in at 2.06 pm on the 89 service from Peterhead. Awaiting to take up their next shifts are HMS242 (NAC93) due to leave for the 4.30 pm 90 circular service and JWG694 (NAC114) the 4.55 pm 89 service to New Deer.

The post-war Alexander single deck body was developed from the 1939 design, modified to accommodate 39 passengers with the TS8 "special" in 1940 and ending with the twenty Leyland OPS2/1 chassis built in 1948 for export to New Zealand. These were DMS814-33 (PB1-20) which were finally licensed in January 1952, only four months before the first Royal Tiger entered service. In 1961, with a requirement for high capacity double deckers, seventeen Leyland PD3s RMS677-93 (MRB245-61) were created from units taken from the PB class fitted into new chassis frames. Their 8' wide bodies were then fitted on to the 7'6" wide chassis from Leyland PS1s with composite bodies requiring renovation. The resulting hybrids thus only had the 7.4 litre engine having donated their 9.8 litre engines to the PD3s, and were condemned to a life of short distance services and school work. DMS820/32-3 in the Fife region escaped conversion. DMS815/9/23-4 (NPB2/6/10-1) passed to Northern with DMS815/9 at Dundee and DMS823-4 at Aberdeen where they regularly alternated at Tarland outstation. DMS824 (NPB11) was transferred to Fyvie Depot in August 1967 and was photographed in Turriff Square on 8th July 1968 on a private hire. It donated units to RMS683 (MRB251) and received the chassis of BWG302 (PA76). Withdrawn in April 1971, it ended up on a farm in Angus.

There were still many half cab single deckers in daily service when Northern was acquiring other operators with a preponderance of underfloor engined vehicles in their fleets, but Montrose Depot was the exception when Mitchell was acquired. While the Alexander bodied AEC Regals and early Leyland PS1s survived until the latter half of the 1960s, there were ten AEC Regals which had bodies constructed at Alexander's bus overhaul works at Brown Street, Falkirk. These were of timber-framed construction, whereas the Alexander bodies built at the factory at Drip Street in Stirling were metal-framed, and being less robust were withdrawn in 1964-65. They resembled the products of Brockhouse of Clydebank, which had supplied bodies for 20 Guy single deckers (G41-8/50-61) due to some of their components being supplied to Falkirk. Mysteriously, G49 was also given one of these bodies. The AECs were AWG629/36-7/9/43-6/8 (NA42/9-50/2/6-9/61) with AWG638 (MA51) having moved from Elgin to Falkirk in February 1961. AWG648 (NA61) was photographed at Montrose Depot in September 1964, and withdrawn for scrap in December 1965. AWG636/43-6 passed to Scottish Omnibuses as their B41-5 at Bathgate.

Although Northern operated throughout the north east of Scotland, there were many small family businesses still providing vital transport links, often based in villages off the main heavily trafficked routes. Such an operator was James Shand at Hamewith, Tarland who operated a service from Tarland to Aboyne Railway Station except on Sundays, although this was reduced to Tuesdays, Fridays and schooldays in the early 1960s. This was a mail and passenger service with a distance of five miles started by Robert Garioch around 1916 and sold to James Shand in September 1948. Photographed outside his garage on 30th May 1965 was Bedford OB DSA896 with a 27 seat SMT body bought new in 1947, still on the premises in 1970 and later identified as a private caravan in Mombasa, Kenya. Inside the garage was CHS895 a 28 seat Mulliner bodied Bedford OB new in February 1947 to Daniel Ferguson of Renfrew, and only recently off the road.

Facing page lower: Still in its original Alexander service bus livery of two tone blue, but with the "& SONS Ltd" removed from the fleet name without the "Northern" being substituted, is Burlingham bodied AEC Regal 1 AMS486 (NA11) emerging from Stonehaven's depot at Arbuthnott Place in August 1963. The workshops were situated here, but the main office and bus stances were on Barclay Street where there was a small garage for eight half cab single deckers. One of twenty, AMS581-90 and AMS486-95 (A1-20) which entered service in 1946, they seated 36 with rear emergency exits whereas the later batch with Burlingham bodies A66-82, had their emergency exits on the offside at the front and seated 35. Introduced at a time when Leyland were unable to supply chassis quickly, with a 7.7 litre engine and crash gear box they proved to be simple and reliable machines. NA6/9-19 passed to Northern in 1961 with NA11 spending its life at Stonehaven Depot, being withdrawn in July 1964 and sold to a dealer in Peterhead in September 1964. It still retains its door at the top of the entrance steps, and the slogan in the ivory cove panel above the windows, but has had its half drop windows replaced by sliding vents. Like the Falkirk-built bodies, it was of timber-framed construction, and thus both Midland and Northern vehicles with Burlingham bodies were withdrawn in 1964 before any of the metal-framed Alexander bodies.

Another local operator providing a connecting service was Gourlay of Victoria Street, Alyth trading as Great and Adam, who ran a service on weekdays from Alyth up Glen Isla to Folda via Dykends, and also services in connection with dances from Alyth to Blairgowrie and to Coupar Angus. Photographed at the garage in Alyth on 11th July 1968 was DES120, an Austin CXB with a 29 seat body built by Mann Egerton of Norwich in March 1950. The business passed to J. McLellan in August 1963 and was renamed Glenisla Coaches. It was still in service in 1972, and passed through Moody's Coaches of Northfleet in Kent to an operator in Belgium and was registered RZV257. In the fleet of "London Ceremony Bus" of Antwerp it was later registered REQ065.

Facing page lower: To the east was James Meffan of Parkend in Kirriemuir who operated from ther up to Brechin via Noranside. Commer GSR244 was photographed on 11th September 1965 parked at the stance at Brechin, waiting to return at 3.30 pm. Its chassis was classified Q4, and dated from 1943 having been supplied to the War Department as a goods chassis which was subsequently reconditioned for PSV use, bringing it up to the standard of the "Commando" which was already available. The light alloy 29 seat coach body was fitted by Scottish Aviation of Prestwick, and the vehicle which was fitted with a Rootes 6 cylinder engine supplied to James Meffan in April 1950. It later acquired a Perkins P6 engine and was the regular vehicle on this service. It was delicensed during winter 1965 for overhaul, and withdrawn in 1968. It passed through the hands of a dealer Heslop in Acomb near Hexham in 1970, later entering preservation and now resides in the Yorkshire Air Museum at Elvington, appearing at rallies in the North East of England.

Further west, Hugh McLachlan who was the proprietor of the hotel at Bridge of Cally, used it as the base for his Burnside Garage, and operated a daily service from Blacklunans down the main A93 through Bridge of Cally to Blairgowrie. At the intersection of Glenshee, Strathardle and Glenericht, Bridge of Cally was strategically located for such a business, but the bus service was taken over by A&C McLennan of Spittalfield in August 1967. A 24 seat Strachan bodied Ford 530E model NES231 was bought in January 1960 to operate this service, but had been disposed of by McLennan by October 1969. I photographed it at Blairgowrie on 29th May 1965 due to depart on the 1.30 pm return journey to Bridge of Cally, unsurprisingly OMO operated. The other vehicle in the fleet was PES231, a Ford 400E model with an eleven-seat Kenex body used on a school contract from Glenshee to Blairgowrie.

Further east was James Bean of Provost Square in Brechin who operated a service from Brechin down to Forfar, as well as schools and three workers' services to Denburn Works, Valley Works and Tool Works. With a fleet of five vehicles, Albions had been favoured in the 1950s, when three new Victors were bought. The first was GSR206, a FT39N model which arrived in September 1949 with a 31 seat body by Federated Industries of Aberdeen, and was withdrawn for scrap by 1965. Similar HSR121 followed in 1951. However, KSR97 which was new in June 1953 was a FT39AN model, and rare in that it had a 1953 season Duple A "Coronation" body seating 33. It was regularly used on the Forfar service, and was photographed on 9th April 1966 on the 1.45 pm service from Forfar. Still in service in 1968, it ended up with Beattie a nearby fruit farmer, for staff transport.

Facing page lower: For full size vehicles, Bean purchased second hand Leyland Tiger PS1 and PS2 models, the first of which was a former Wallace Arnold Leyland PS1/1 KUM833 new in August 1947 with a 33 seat Burlingham coach body, and photographed outside the garage at Brechin on 11th September 1965. As was their habit, it was modernised by in this case replacing it with a 1950 vintage Burlingham Sun Saloon body in 1953. This had come from an AEC Regal 111 NUA785 in one of Wallace Arnold's complex body exchanges. It passed to Bean in March 1961 and was principally used on school services together with another ex-Wallace Arnold coach (NUA751) which had also been modernised. It was a Leyland PS2/3 new in 1950 with a Burlingham Sun Saloon body from the same batch as above. However it was re-bodied by Plaxton in January 1953 with a full-front 35 seat body, and the chassis subsequently extended to 30' to accommodate 37 seats. It arrived from Mitchell of Luthermuir in September 1962, and was withdrawn in 1968, but KUM833 survived until 1970.

Another Burlingham Sun Saloon bodied Leyland Tiger to operate in the area was HDK801, one of a pair (HDK801-2) of PS2/3 models new to Yelloway Motor Services of Rochdale in February 1951 with 37 seat coach bodies, and acquired by A&C MacLennan of Spittalfield in May 1962 and April 1962 respectively. They were both later reseated to 39, and principally operated OMO out of the small depot at Blairgowrie, being withdrawn in 1968. HDK801 was photographed on 18th April 1966 leaving the village of Ballintuim on service from Kirkmichael to Blairgowrie via Bridge of Cally. The service had been started in 1919 by John Harper of Blairgowrie who was awarded a mail bus contract starting from the village of Enochdhu two miles north of Kirkmichael, and Maclennan still operated a single daily run from there.

Further north at Braemar Sub-depot, Northern regularly garaged one of its Leyland PS1s with Burlingham Sun Saloon bodies during 1966 and 1967, for the first run of the day at 7.00am into Ballater, returning at 5.40 pm. When Strachan's was taken over on 3rd May 1965, Northern immediately drafted in CWG334-6 (NPA207-9) which had already been converted for OMO operation the previous October, having been transferred in to Aberdeen from Macduff and Dundee depots. As such, they had been operating a three day cycle, outstationed at the villages of Lumphanan and Strathdon, and returning to Aberdeen Depot on the third night. However, they proved to be good replacements for the Fodens at Ballater, and remained there for the next three years. They had entered service in 1950 as part of the delayed order for sixteen PS1s, CWG330-43 (PA203-16) which arrived with Burlingham rather than the customary Alexander bodies and were split between Northern and Fife, with CWG330-6/9/41 going north. However, with heavy steering and sliding doors, they were not popular for service work, and tended to be used on hires and contract work. CWG334 (NPA207) was parked at the entrance to the depot in Ballater, beside Strachans Foden GSA303 on 23rd April 1965 as preparations were being made for the take over.

Facing page upper: Initially, they were regularly used on the Crathie school service which was OMO operated and in the timetable as route number 1A, and had historically been operated by Alexander. It was renumbered 1D after the Strachan's services were absorbed, and CWG336 (NPA209) was photographed at Ballater Station on the same day waiting to take up its run at 4 pm. Just parked behind is AEC Reliance NMS509 (NAC166) on its regular roster on the 2.15 1 service from Aberdeen to Braemar. Before Strachan's was taken over, Ballater Railway Station was the departure point for the Alexander services, and there was an office in the station building, with the three buses being garaged overnight in a carriage shed behind. The train tickets had even been interchangeable with those on Alexanders buses. The station was opened by The Great North of Scotland Railway on October 17th 1866 at the terminus of the service from Aberdeen, although the track was built as far as Bridge of Gairn. It was closed on 28th February 1966 when the service was axed during the "Beeching Cuts," but a visitor centre was developed, and there are plans to reinstate this following a disastrous fire on 12th May 1915. CWG336 in fact swapped with Bedford SRS134 at Huntly Depot, and CWG334 moved to Forfar and CWG335 to Blairgowrie in 1969. All of the Northern ones were withdrawn in 1971, whereas the five which went to Fife were all off the road by 1965.

Most of the former Sutherland's all-Leyland PD1As (NRA90-101) which Northern acquired in 1950 later moved south from their original depots in Buchan where NRA90-5 were allocated to Rosehearty and NRA96-101 based at Peterhead. The first to leave were NRA92-6 transferred to Aberdeen in 1956 followed by NRA90-1 in 1957 as 45 seat Alexander bodied service buses came new to the northern region. Initially they were a mixture of AEC Reliances and Monocoaches, and also Leyland Tiger Cubs from the batch GWG267-96 (PD41-70) of which fourteen came north with PD47-50/62 allocated to Peterhead. However, they all went south when the 1956 batch of AEC Reliances (NAC81-99) all entered service in the northern region in August 1956. NRA97-8 later came to Aberdeen in January 1960, and in 1962 NRA95-7 moved down to Stonehaven where they remained until withdrawn in 1970 (NRA96-7) and in January 1971 (NRA95). At Stonehaven the trio were used on peak hour and duplicate runs to Aberdeen as well as school services, and were photographed at Aberdeen Bus Station on 25th August 1963 showing detailed differences in appearance.

When NRA92-6 first came down to Aberdeen Depot, they were used on the services out to Methlick via Udny Green and Cairnbrogie, but when this photograph was taken on 3rd October 1961, only one was parked outside Methlick garage overnight with the three single deckers inside. The location was Mealmarket Street, the departure point for services heading north out of Aberdeen, and NRA91 is waiting to take up its regular return journey on the 5.45 pm 69A service to Methlick via Udny Green. With only four months since the split up of the parent Alexander company, it shows no indication of its new owner, and had not been significantly rebuilt at this time. This rear view shows the neat way in which the emergency exit has been incorporated into the rear platform with the door, a specification which James Sutherland routinely included in every new double decker order since 1938. NRA91 was withdrawn after an accident in May 1968 and dismantled for spares, but the remainder at Aberdeen were dispersed in July 1968, with NRA98 returning north. When it first moved down with NRA97, there was a piece in the local paper about buses without any platform door being used on the local service from Peterhead to Boddam, as the pair were replaced by new 67 seat Leyland PD3s NWG903/5 (NRB214/6). This had apparently caused some consternation among local people used to double deckers with platform doors to provide protection from the blustery weather.

Facing page lower: The other utility Daimlers still in service in the North East were Aberdeen Corporation CWA6s which had all been heavily rebuilt in their workshops between 1957 and 1960, and make an interesting comparison with CAV825 above. All were still in daily service when I took this photograph at the Corporation's depot in King Street on 23rd April 1965. The line-up included BRG917 (141) BRS29 (147) BRG916 (140) BRG950 (144) and BRG935 (142) all with Duple bodies apart from 144 with a Brush body, with 147 being to the relaxed Ministry of Supply specification. They were all withdrawn later that year apart from 140 which survived until 1966, and all were sold to dealers for scrap.

Even the wartime allocation of Guys and Daimlers to the Sutherland fleet arrived with platform doors, and while the nine Guys (RO672-80) were promptly transferred south after the takeover, the ten Daimler CWA6s CAV314/595/824-6/97-9 and CSA342-3 (RO681-90) remained to join the Northern fleet, but were all transferred to Midland in 1962. Their bodywork was by Duple, apart from RO681 by Brush and 689-90 by Massey, and during the 1950s, RO681-3/5/7-90 were allocated to Peterhead. RO686 was at Aberdeen, but kept at Ellon overnight and was accorded the title of the "Ellon Special" for its commuter run in to Aberdeen. RO684 allocated to Rosehearty was outstationed at New Pitsligo for the 69B service to Fraserburgh, and I photographed it at Fraserburgh on 4th October 1961, as the driver was changing the screen for its return journey. With the design of its platform door, the emergency exit has been located to the front of the lower offside windows, and the body shows signs of its past extensive rebuild at Gairn Terrace with new window panes. Parked beside it is Duple re-bodied Leyland TS7 ASF388 (NP837). Apart from the Massey bodied pair, the other Peterhead allocated Daimlers were by then all delicensed. CAV825 (RO684) moved south to Kilsyth Depot in January 1962 and was withdrawn on 30th September 1964. Parked beside it is Duple bodied Leyland PS1 EAV636 (NPA201) still in Bluebird livery.

Burnetts of Mintlaw favoured local products for its new purchases until 1951 with Albion being the choice for its single deckers with bodywork by Cowieson before the war, and Pickering, Federated Industries and Walker of Aberdeen in the post-war period. They also ordered bodies by Federated Industries, also based in Aberdeen, for a couple of AEC Regents in 1950, and had single deckers overhauled and re-bodied by them and by Walker. However, it was to Burlingham that they turned in 1953, when the original Pickering bodies on Albion CX13 CSA146 and CSA172 required remedial work, and they were fitted with new 35 seat Sun Saloon bodies. They continued in service for another twelve years whereas the other pair from the 1946 intake, CSA145 and CSA173 were withdrawn in December 1959. CSA172 was photographed on 30th May 1965 at the depot in Mintlaw just nine months before it was withdrawn, but CSA146 was already delicensed. Parked beside it is Park Royal bodied AEC Regent 111 OFC378 which had arrived from the City of Oxford Motor Services in December 1963 and fitted with platform doors by Burnett before entering service, although it was to be another twenty months before it passed to Northern. This garage was formerly used by Scottish Agricultural industries and passed to Northern, whereas the Burnett premises on South Street were retained for the haulage side of the business.